PREVIEW

Between Certainty and Doubt is an intellectual journey through the intricate space between belief and skepticism. Drawing on a wide range of philosophical works and thinkers, from Descartes and Kant to Kierkegaard and Sartre, this book offers a rich exploration of how certainty and doubt shape our understanding of the world. With references to major philosophical texts and ideas, it delves into the nature of truth, knowledge, and personal growth. Ideal for readers who seek to challenge their perspectives, this book weaves together timeless wisdom with contemporary insights on navigating the unknown.

Table of content

BETWEEN CERTAINTY AND DOUBT

A SEARCH FOR MEANING

Jeet.p

Chapter 1: The Space Between Certainty and Doubt

Human beings have always sought meaning. From the dawn of civilization, we have yearned to understand the world around us and our place within it. This search for meaning has led to the birth of philosophy, religion, science, and art—each, in its own way, an attempt to provide answers to the fundamental questions of existence. At the heart of this search lies a tension that has shaped human thought across time and cultures: the tension between certainty and doubt. On the one hand, certainty provides a sense of security, a grounding in truth that allows us to navigate the world confidently. On the other hand, doubt is the seed of curiosity, the force that propels us to question, to explore, and to challenge the very foundations of what we think we know. It is in the space between these two poles—certainty and doubt—that the human search for meaning unfolds.

Certainty is often seen as a desirable state, one that offers stability and clarity. The feeling of knowing something with confidence, of having a firm grasp on reality, can be deeply comforting. In philosophy, certainty has been a central concern since the time of the ancient Greeks. Plato, for example, believed in the existence of absolute truths—unchanging, eternal forms that could be known through reason. For Plato, knowledge was not something that fluctuated with the whims of opinion or perception; it was something stable, something one could attain with certainty through intellectual contemplation. This Platonic ideal of certainty as something unshakable and eternal laid the groundwork for much of Western philosophical thought.

Aristotle, Plato's student, also sought certainty, though his approach was more grounded in empirical observation than in abstract reasoning. For Aristotle, certainty could be found in the careful study of the natural world. By observing patterns, categorizing phenomena, and employing logic, Aristotle believed we could arrive at knowledge that was reliable and certain. This emphasis on observation and reason would eventually influence the development of the scientific method, which seeks certainty through evidence and experimentation.

In the modern era, the quest for certainty took on new dimensions with the rise of scientific inquiry. The scientific revolution, which began in the 16th century, marked a shift in the way human beings sought knowledge. Thinkers like Galileo, Newton, and later, Einstein, sought to uncover the laws governing the universe, believing that with enough observation and analysis, the mysteries of the world could be fully understood. This era of scientific optimism was built on the assumption that certainty was attainable through the rigorous application of reason and empirical evidence.

Yet, alongside this drive for certainty, doubt has always played an equally important role in the search for meaning. Doubt is the force that challenges the status quo, the questioning spirit that refuses to accept easy answers. In the philosophical tradition, doubt is not a sign of weakness or ignorance; rather, it is a necessary part of the process of inquiry. Socrates, one of the founders of Western philosophy, famously said, "I know that I know nothing." This statement captures the essence of philosophical doubt: a recognition that true wisdom lies in acknowledging the limits of one's knowledge.

Socratic doubt is not about rejecting knowledge altogether; rather, it is about remaining open to the possibility that our beliefs may be incomplete or mistaken. Socrates' method of questioning, known as the Socratic method, involved systematically probing the assumptions and beliefs of his interlocutors, revealing contradictions and gaps in their reasoning. By doing so, Socrates demonstrated that doubt could lead to deeper understanding. It is through doubt that we refine our beliefs and approach a clearer, more accurate understanding of the truth.

In the 17th century, René Descartes, one of the key figures of modern philosophy, elevated doubt to a methodological principle. In his famous work *Meditations on First Philosophy*, Descartes set out to find a foundation for knowledge that could not be doubted. He famously declared, "Cogito, ergo sum"—"I think, therefore I am." Descartes' radical doubt led him to the conclusion that the only thing he could be absolutely certain of was his own existence as a thinking being. Everything else, he argued, could be subject to doubt. Descartes' method of systematic doubt laid the groundwork for modern philosophy's emphasis on skepticism and the search for foundational truths.

While doubt can be unsettling, it is also profoundly liberating. Doubt frees us from the constraints of dogma and opens up the possibility of new ways of thinking. It challenges us to question not only the external world but also our own assumptions and biases. In this sense, doubt is a creative force, one that pushes us to explore the unknown and expand the boundaries of our understanding.

However, doubt can also be paralyzing. When taken to an extreme, doubt can lead to skepticism or nihilism, where one questions the very possibility of knowing anything with certainty. This is the danger of unchecked doubt: it can erode our confidence in the existence of meaning altogether. If everything is uncertain, if all knowledge is provisional and subject to change, then where do we find solid ground? How do we live meaningfully in a world where doubt pervades our every thought?

This tension between certainty and doubt is not just an abstract philosophical problem; it is a deeply human one. It shapes our personal lives, our relationships, and our understanding of the world. In moments of crisis, we may find ourselves clinging to certainty as a way of coping with uncertainty and chaos. At other times, we may embrace doubt as a necessary step toward growth and transformation. The search for meaning is a dynamic process that involves both the desire for certainty and the willingness to engage with doubt.

Religious traditions have long grappled with the interplay between certainty and doubt. Faith, by its very nature, involves a degree of certainty—a belief in something that transcends empirical evidence. For many, religious faith provides a sense of meaning and purpose that is grounded in certainty. Yet, even within religious traditions, doubt plays an important role. Theologians and mystics throughout history have spoken of the "dark night of the soul," a period of spiritual doubt and uncertainty that is often seen as a necessary phase in the journey toward deeper faith.

In the modern secular world, where traditional sources of meaning—such as religion and community—have often been displaced by individualism and scientific rationality, the tension between certainty and doubt is perhaps more pronounced than ever. Many people find themselves searching for meaning in a world where the old certainties no longer hold. The rise of existentialism in the 20th century reflects this shift. Thinkers like Jean-Paul Sartre and Albert Camus explored the human condition in a world devoid of inherent meaning, where individuals are free to create their own meaning, but must also confront the void of uncertainty.

Sartre's famous declaration that "existence precedes essence" encapsulates this modern existential dilemma. For Sartre, there is no preordained meaning or purpose to life; we are thrust into existence without a script, and it is up to us to create meaning through our choices and actions. This freedom, while exhilarating, is also terrifying, as it places the burden of meaning-making squarely on the individual. In this sense, existentialism embraces both certainty and doubt: certainty in the sense that we are free to create meaning, but doubt in the sense that there is no external guarantee that the meaning we create is valid or lasting.

The existentialist's confrontation with the absurd—the recognition that life has no inherent meaning, yet we must go on living and seeking meaning—is a powerful illustration of the tension between certainty and doubt. Camus, in his essay *The Myth of Sisyphus*, compares human existence to the plight of Sisyphus, the figure from Greek mythology who is condemned to roll a boulder up a hill, only for it to roll back down each time he reaches the top. For Camus, the key to living meaningfully in the face of absurdity is to embrace the struggle, to find joy and meaning in the act of pushing the boulder, even though the outcome is uncertain and the task seems futile.

This idea of finding meaning in the process rather than the outcome resonates with many contemporary thinkers. In a world where rapid technological advancements, political upheavals, and environmental crises make the future increasingly uncertain, the search for meaning often involves embracing uncertainty and learning to live with doubt. Rather than seeking fixed answers, we may find meaning in the ongoing search itself—in the questions we ask, the relationships we build, and the experiences we cultivate.

As we navigate this space between certainty and doubt, we are constantly shaping our understanding of meaning. Certainty provides a sense of stability, grounding us in a reality we can trust, while doubt keeps us open to new possibilities and deeper truths. It is the interplay between these two forces that drives human inquiry, creativity, and growth.

In the chapters that follow, we will explore how different philosophical traditions, cultural narratives, and personal experiences grapple with the tension between certainty and doubt. We will examine how this tension shapes our understanding of knowledge, ethics, identity, and purpose. Ultimately, the search for meaning is not about resolving the tension between certainty and doubt, but about learning to live within it—embracing the questions, seeking the answers, and finding meaning in the space between.

Chapter 2: The Certainty of Existence – Philosophical Foundations

Throughout history, the human desire for certainty has been a powerful force driving intellectual exploration and philosophical inquiry. Certainty represents the ultimate goal for those who seek to ground their understanding of reality in something stable and unchanging. The quest for certainty is not merely an abstract intellectual exercise—it is a fundamental aspect of the human experience. We seek certainty in our knowledge, in our relationships, and in our purpose because it provides a foundation upon which we can build our lives.

From the earliest days of Western philosophy, thinkers have grappled with the problem of certainty. One of the earliest and most influential figures to address this issue was Plato. For Plato, certainty could be found in the realm of abstract forms, which he believed were the ultimate reality behind the ever-changing world of appearances. Plato's theory of forms posited that the physical world we perceive with our senses is merely a shadow of a higher, more perfect reality. According to Plato, the forms are eternal and unchanging, existing outside of time and space. While the physical world is subject to change and decay, the forms remain constant, and it is through the contemplation of these forms that we can attain true knowledge and certainty.

Plato illustrated this idea in his famous allegory of the cave, where prisoners are chained in a dark cave, facing a wall upon which shadows are cast by objects behind them. The prisoners, who can only see the shadows, mistake them for reality. It is only when one prisoner escapes the cave and sees the objects themselves—and, eventually, the sun—that he comes to understand the true nature of reality. For Plato, the world of appearances is like the cave, while the forms represent the higher reality that can be known only through reason and intellectual insight. Certainty, then, is not found in the sensory world, but in the realm of abstract thought.

This Platonic view of certainty as something beyond the physical world had a profound influence on later philosophical and religious thought. In particular, it shaped the development of Christian theology in the early centuries of the common era. Christian thinkers, such as Augustine and Aquinas, drew on Platonic and Aristotelian ideas to articulate their own views on the nature of certainty, grounding it in the divine.

For Augustine, certainty could be found in the existence of God and in the divine order that governs the universe. In his *Confessions*, Augustine reflects on his own journey from doubt to faith, concluding that true certainty can only be found in God, who is the source of all truth and knowledge. Augustine's belief in divine certainty was rooted in the idea that human beings are created in the image of God and, therefore, have the capacity to know divine truths through faith and reason. However, this certainty is not the same as empirical knowledge—it is a certainty grounded in faith, which transcends the limitations of human reason.

Aquinas, building on both Augustine and Aristotle, sought to reconcile faith and reason by arguing that certain truths could be known through reason alone (natural theology), while others could only be known through divine revelation. Aquinas believed that the existence of God, for example, could be demonstrated through logical arguments, such as the famous *Five Ways,* which provided rational proofs for the existence of God based on observation of the natural world. For Aquinas, certainty about the existence of God could be attained both through reason and through faith, with the two working in harmony.

While the medieval period was marked by a strong emphasis on religious certainty, the dawn of the modern era brought new challenges to the idea of certainty, particularly in the realm of science and philosophy. The 17th century saw the rise of a new kind of doubt—one that questioned the very foundations of knowledge itself. This period, known as the Age of Enlightenment, was characterized by a shift away from reliance on religious authority and toward a reliance on reason and empirical observation as the primary sources of knowledge.

René Descartes, often considered the father of modern philosophy, played a pivotal role in this shift. Descartes' project was to find a foundation for knowledge that was absolutely certain, and he famously did this by subjecting all of his beliefs to radical doubt. In his *Meditations on First Philosophy*, Descartes systematically doubted everything he had previously taken for granted: the reliability of the senses, the existence of the physical world, and even the existence of his own body. Descartes' method of doubt led him to question whether anything could be known with certainty.

However, Descartes did not remain in doubt indefinitely. Through his process of radical skepticism, Descartes arrived at one thing that he believed could not be doubted: the existence of his own mind. His famous conclusion, "Cogito, ergo sum" ("I think, therefore I am"), represents the first certainty that Descartes believed he could attain. No matter how much he doubted, Descartes reasoned, he could not doubt the fact that he was doubting, and therefore, he must exist as a thinking being.

For Descartes, this realization provided the foundation upon which he could rebuild his understanding of the world. From the certainty of his own existence, Descartes proceeded to argue for the existence of God, reasoning that the idea of a perfect being must have been placed in his mind by such a being, since a finite, imperfect human being could not have conceived of perfection on his own. Descartes also used the existence of God to argue for the reliability of the senses, claiming that a benevolent God would not deceive him by creating a world that did not correspond to his sensory perceptions.

Descartes' quest for certainty was groundbreaking in its method and conclusions, but it also sparked a series of debates and challenges that would shape the development of modern philosophy. One of the most significant responses to Descartes came from the empiricist tradition, particularly through the work of John Locke, George Berkeley, and David Hume. These thinkers rejected Descartes' emphasis on reason as the sole source of knowledge and instead argued that knowledge arises primarily from sensory experience.

John Locke, in his *Essay Concerning Human Understanding*, argued that the human mind is a "tabula rasa" (blank slate) at birth, and all knowledge comes from experience. For Locke, certainty was attainable through the careful observation of the world, and he distinguished between different types of knowledge: intuitive knowledge (which is immediate and self-evident), demonstrative knowledge (which requires reasoning), and sensitive knowledge (which comes from sensory experience). Locke believed that while some knowledge, such as mathematical truths, could be known with certainty, much of what we know about the external world is based on probable reasoning rather than absolute certainty.

George Berkeley took Locke's empiricism a step further by arguing that the external world does not exist independently of our perceptions. In his *Principles of Human Knowledge*, Berkeley famously declared that "to be is to be perceived" (esseest percipi). For Berkeley, the objects we perceive do not exist outside of our minds; rather, they exist as ideas in the mind of God, who guarantees the stability and consistency of our perceptions. While Berkeley's view was radical, it reflected a deep concern with the nature of certainty and the reliability of human perception.

David Hume, perhaps the most skeptical of the empiricists, challenged the very possibility of certainty in human knowledge. In his *An Enquiry Concerning Human Understanding*, Hume argued that all of our knowledge about the world is based on habit and custom rather than on any rational certainty. According to Hume, we cannot know with certainty that the sun will rise tomorrow, even though we expect it to, because our expectations are based on past experience rather than on any logical necessity. Hume's skepticism extended to questions of causality, personal identity, and the existence of God, leading him to conclude that much of what we take for granted as certain is, in fact, based on mere belief rather than knowledge.

The empiricist challenge to certainty had profound implications for the development of modern thought, particularly in the realm of science. The scientific revolution, which began in the 16th century with figures like Galileo and Newton, was driven by the search for certainty through empirical observation and experimentation. The scientific method, which involves formulating hypotheses, testing them through observation and experimentation, and drawing conclusions based on evidence, became the standard for acquiring knowledge in the natural world.

However, the rise of science also brought with it new uncertainties. As scientists probed deeper into the mysteries of the universe, they discovered that many of the certainties that had been taken for granted in classical physics were not as solid as they had appeared. The development of quantum mechanics in the early 20th century, for example, revealed that at the subatomic level, particles do not behave in predictable ways. Instead, they exist in a state of uncertainty, governed by probabilities rather than by deterministic laws. This "quantum uncertainty" challenged the classical view of a predictable, clockwork universe and introduced a new kind of uncertainty into the realm of scientific knowledge.

In the realm of psychology, too, the quest for certainty has faced significant challenges. Sigmund Freud, the founder of psychoanalysis, argued that much of human behavior is driven by unconscious desires and impulses that are not accessible to the conscious mind. For Freud, certainty about one's own thoughts and motivations is often an illusion, as the unconscious mind exerts a powerful influence on behavior without our awareness. This idea has been expanded upon by later psychologists and neuroscientists, who have demonstrated that much of human cognition operates at an unconscious level, raising questions about the extent to which we can ever be certain about our own thoughts, emotions, and decisions.

As we move further into the 21st century, the quest for certainty continues to evolve. Advances in artificial intelligence, neuroscience, and cosmology have opened up new frontiers of knowledge, but they have also raised new uncertainties. In a world where information is constantly changing, where scientific theories are revised and updated, and where technology is advancing at a rapid pace, the search for certainty may seem more elusive than ever.

Yet, despite the challenges and uncertainties we face, the human desire for certainty remains. Whether through philosophy, science, religion, or personal experience, we continue to seek stable ground in a world that is often unpredictable and uncertain. The search for certainty is not just an intellectual pursuit—it is a deeply human one, driven

by our need to make sense of the world and our place within
it.

Chapter 3: The Power of Doubt – Embracing Uncertainty

The exploration of doubt is as ancient as the search for
certainty. Throughout human history, from philosophy to
religion, doubt has played a critical role in shaping our
understanding of the world, ourselves, and the divine. Doubt
is not simply the absence of belief but a powerful force that
compels us to question, challenge, and, ultimately, grow. In
this chapter, we will explore the philosophical and spiritual
dimensions of doubt, its transformative power, and how it
functions not only in Western philosophy but also in the rich
narratives of the *Ramayana* and the *Mahabharata*—two of
the most important epics in Hindu tradition.

The Philosophical Significance of Doubt

Doubt has been the catalyst for many of the greatest
intellectual and spiritual breakthroughs. In Western
philosophy, doubt has often been seen as a tool for achieving
deeper truth. For Socrates, doubt was the cornerstone of his
philosophical practice. His method, known as the Socratic
method, was based on asking probing questions to reveal the
ignorance or inconsistencies in his interlocutors' beliefs.
Rather than providing answers, Socrates insisted that
genuine wisdom comes from recognizing one's own
ignorance. His assertion, *"I know that I know nothing,"*

highlighted how doubt is the beginning of all wisdom. It was through doubt that Socrates encouraged his students to question the assumptions they held about justice, virtue, and the nature of the good life.

René Descartes, as discussed in the previous chapter, brought doubt to the forefront of philosophical inquiry. By systematically doubting everything, from the reliability of the senses to the existence of the external world, Descartes aimed to find something that could not be doubted. His famous conclusion, *"Cogito, ergo sum"* ("I think, therefore I am"), was his ultimate response to the doubt he created. Yet, despite Descartes' attempt to escape doubt, his philosophy illustrated how crucial doubt is to the very process of seeking certainty.

Descartes' radical doubt pushed the boundaries of what could be known, but it also opened up a more profound understanding: that doubt itself is a necessary part of the search for meaning. By questioning the beliefs we hold most dear, doubt clears the ground for new insights and deeper understanding. It allows us to move beyond superficial explanations and engage with life's complexities in a more meaningful way.

Doubt in the *Ramayana*: Rama's Moral Dilemmas

In the Indian epic *Ramayana*, doubt plays a central role in some of the most morally and emotionally charged moments of the narrative. While the *Ramayana* is often seen as a story of duty, righteousness, and devotion, it is also a story of profound internal conflict, where doubt forces the characters to grapple with difficult choices.

One of the most significant moments of doubt in the *Ramayana* occurs after Lord Rama rescues his wife, Sita, from the demon king Ravana. Despite Sita's unwavering loyalty and purity during her captivity, Rama publicly questions her chastity and demands that she prove her fidelity by undergoing the trial of fire, known as *Agni Pariksha*. Although Sita passes the test, Rama's doubt reveals a deeper tension between his personal love for Sita and his sense of duty as a king. Rama is caught between his responsibility to his kingdom, which demands that he uphold social conventions, and his personal feelings of trust and affection for his wife.

Rama's doubt serves as a reflection of the tension between certainty and doubt in human relationships. Even the ideal king and husband, revered as an incarnation of Vishnu, cannot escape the weight of doubt. His decision, rooted in social expectations, is a reminder that doubt can lead to painful but necessary questioning of deeply held beliefs. The doubt that Rama feels is not a sign of weakness but a powerful indication of the complexity of human emotions and moral dilemmas.

This episode forces us to reflect on how doubt shapes our ethical decisions. It challenges the simplistic notion of certainty in moral judgment, reminding us that human experience is fraught with ambiguity. Rama's doubt and subsequent decision highlight the ongoing struggle between personal convictions and societal expectations—a tension that continues to resonate in modern life.

Doubt in the *Mahabharata*: Arjuna's Crisis of Conscience

The *Mahabharata,* another monumental Indian epic, is filled with characters grappling with doubt, none more famously than Arjuna, the warrior prince. At the heart of the *Mahabharata* lies the Bhagavad Gita, a philosophical dialogue between Arjuna and Krishna, which is sparked by Arjuna's profound existential doubt.

On the battlefield of Kurukshetra, as Arjuna prepares to lead his family into war, he is overwhelmed by doubt. He questions the morality of the impending battle and the righteousness of fighting against his own kin. Arjuna's doubt is not just about the immediate act of violence but about the deeper consequences of his actions. He wonders whether the pursuit of victory, power, and dharma (duty) is worth the destruction of his family and the bloodshed that will follow.

Arjuna's internal struggle mirrors the tension between certainty and doubt that permeates human existence. Caught between his duty as a warrior and his compassion as a human being, Arjuna is paralyzed by indecision. His doubt leads him to question the very foundations of his identity and purpose. This moment of deep crisis is transformative; it forces Arjuna to confront not only the ethics of warfare but also the nature of life, death, and the eternal soul.

In response to Arjuna's doubt, Krishna imparts the wisdom of the Bhagavad Gita. Rather than dismissing Arjuna's doubts, Krishna acknowledges them as a necessary part of spiritual growth. Krishna teaches Arjuna that doubt, while painful, can be the gateway to wisdom. He explains that true understanding comes from seeing beyond the dualities of life—victory and defeat, pleasure and pain, life and death.

Krishna urges Arjuna to rise above his doubt by embracing a higher perspective: the eternal self, which remains untouched by worldly conflict.

The dialogue between Arjuna and Krishna highlights the essential role of doubt in spiritual and ethical development. Arjuna's doubts are not resolved by simple answers; instead, they lead him to a deeper understanding of duty, detachment, and the nature of the self. The Gita shows us that doubt can be a powerful force for transformation, pushing us to question our assumptions and leading us toward a more profound understanding of life's complexities.

Doubt as a Catalyst for Growth

Both the *Ramayana* and the *Mahabharata* illustrate how doubt is not something to be feared or avoided but embraced as a critical part of the human experience. Doubt can be uncomfortable, especially when it challenges long-held beliefs or forces us to confront difficult choices. Yet, as seen in the dilemmas of Rama and Arjuna, doubt often leads to deeper reflection, growth, and ultimately, transformation.

In a world where certainty is often elusive, doubt can serve as a powerful catalyst for intellectual, moral, and spiritual development. It encourages us to remain open to new perspectives, to question our assumptions, and to seek truth even when the path is uncertain. Rather than clinging to certainty as a source of security, embracing doubt allows us to engage more fully with the complexities of existence.

Doubt also helps us cultivate humility. It reminds us that our knowledge is limited and that the world is far more intricate than our understanding of it. This humility, in turn, fosters empathy—allowing us to see the world through the eyes of others, to understand different viewpoints, and to appreciate the richness of human experience.

In the search for meaning, doubt is not the enemy of certainty but its complement. Just as night gives way to day, doubt often precedes moments of clarity and insight. By embracing uncertainty, we open ourselves to a deeper, more authentic engagement with life. Rather than seeking rigid answers, we learn to navigate the ever-shifting landscape of human existence with curiosity, openness, and a willingness to grow.

Chapter 4: The Interplay of Doubt and Certainty in Ancient Indian Thought

In our exploration of doubt and certainty, we have so far seen how these two forces shape philosophical, ethical, and spiritual inquiries in the human search for meaning. In this chapter, we turn to ancient India, where the interplay between doubt and certainty was not only a significant part of intellectual life but also a driving force behind some of the most profound contributions to philosophy, spirituality, and science.

Ancient India was a land of philosophical diversity, where different schools of thought engaged with each other in debates that spanned centuries. The Indian intellectual tradition was not monolithic; it was a rich tapestry of ideas that ranged from the rational skepticism of the *Lokayata* (Charvaka) materialists to the spiritual certainties of the Vedic sages and the meditative insights of the Buddha. Through examples from the Upanishads, the Buddha's teachings, and the *Nyaya* and *Charvaka* schools, we will explore how ancient Indian thought grappled with the tension between certainty and doubt.

The Upanishads: Seeking Certainty Through Introspection

The Upanishads, a collection of spiritual and philosophical texts that emerged in the late Vedic period, are among the earliest attempts in ancient India to grapple with profound existential questions. They form the basis of what we now call Vedanta philosophy and deal with the nature of reality, the self, and the ultimate purpose of life. The sages of the Upanishads were not content with the ritualistic practices of the Vedic tradition, which focused on appeasing the gods through elaborate sacrifices. Instead, they turned inward, seeking certainty about the nature of the self (Atman) and its relationship with the ultimate reality (Brahman).

The Upanishads represent a deep quest for certainty, but they also contain an inherent acknowledgment of doubt. The sages questioned the value of external rituals and instead sought a direct experience of the divine. This shift from external religious practices to internal contemplation illustrates the tension between doubt and certainty in the search for truth. One of the most famous passages from the *Chandogya Upanishad* is the dialogue between the sage Uddalaka and his son Svetaketu, where Uddalaka teaches his son that the ultimate truth, Brahman, is not something that can be known through rituals or external knowledge but through self-realization.

In this passage, Uddalaka uses the analogy of salt dissolved in water to explain the nature of Brahman. Just as the presence of salt in water cannot be seen but can be tasted, Brahman permeates all things, though it cannot be perceived by the senses. This teaching pushes Svetaketu to move beyond his limited understanding of reality and question the knowledge he has accumulated through traditional education. The

Upanishads thus encourage doubt in superficial knowledge and certainty in the deeper truths that can only be realized through introspection and meditation.

However, the certainty of the Upanishadic sages was not easily won. Their path involved a rigorous process of doubt, questioning, and self-inquiry. The famous phrase from the *Brihadaranyaka Upanishad*, "Neti, neti" (not this, not this), exemplifies this process. The sages used this method to strip away all false certainties and superficial identities, denying everything that the self is not in order to arrive at the true essence of the self. In this sense, doubt was a crucial tool in the Upanishadic search for certainty.

The Buddha: Radical Doubt as a Path to Enlightenment

Perhaps the most radical expression of doubt in ancient India came from Siddhartha Gautama, the Buddha. The Buddha's entire spiritual journey can be understood as a response to doubt. Born into a life of privilege and certainty, the young prince Siddhartha was shielded from the harsh realities of life until his encounters with old age, sickness, and death shattered his illusions of worldly certainty. These experiences ignited a profound existential doubt that led him to abandon his life of comfort and seek the truth about suffering and the nature of existence.

The Buddha's path to enlightenment was paved with doubt. He questioned the validity of the extreme ascetic practices of his time, which advocated severe physical deprivation as a means of spiritual progress. Rejecting both the indulgence of his princely life and the extreme asceticism of the forest sages, the Buddha embraced the "Middle Way," a path of moderation. His doubt in both these extremes led him to develop his own path of meditation and insight, which eventually culminated in his awakening.

The Buddha's teachings in the *Dhamma* also reflect this deep engagement with doubt. Rather than encouraging blind faith, the Buddha urged his followers to question everything, even his own teachings. In the famous *Kalama Sutta*, the Buddha advises the Kalamas, a group of villagers, not to accept teachings based on tradition, authority, or hearsay. Instead, he encourages them to investigate for themselves and only accept what they find to be true through their own experience. This emphasis on personal experience over external authority reflects the central role that doubt played in the Buddha's path to certainty.

The Buddha's teachings on *anicca* (impermanence), *dukkha* (suffering), and *anatta* (non-self) further illustrate his rejection of absolute certainties. According to the Buddha, all things are impermanent, and attachment to fixed identities or beliefs leads to suffering. The concept of *anatta*, in particular, challenges the idea of a permanent, unchanging self, which was a central tenet of many Indian philosophical schools. By rejecting the notion of a permanent self, the Buddha introduced a radical form of doubt into the spiritual landscape of ancient India. Yet, paradoxically, it was this very doubt that led to the realization of *nirvana*, a state of profound certainty and liberation from the cycle of suffering.

The *Nyaya* School: Reason and Logic as Paths to Certainty

While the Upanishads and the Buddha emphasized introspection and meditation, the *Nyaya* school of philosophy developed a rigorous system of logic and epistemology to address the question of certainty. The *Nyaya* philosophers believed that knowledge could be attained through a combination of perception, inference, comparison, and verbal testimony. Their approach was deeply analytical, and they developed a sophisticated theory of knowledge that aimed to establish certainty through reasoned argument.

For the *Nyaya* school, doubt (*samsaya*) was seen as a legitimate and necessary stage in the process of gaining knowledge. Doubt was the starting point for inquiry, and it had to be resolved through careful reasoning and analysis. The *Nyaya Sutras*, attributed to the sage Gautama (not to be confused with the Buddha), outline methods for resolving doubt through logical debate and systematic investigation.

The *Nyaya* school's emphasis on doubt as a precursor to certainty mirrors the Socratic method in Western philosophy, where questioning and doubt are seen as necessary steps toward deeper understanding. However, the *Nyaya* philosophers also acknowledged the limitations of human reasoning and the potential for error in perception and inference. As a result, they developed detailed rules for logical argumentation, designed to minimize error and lead to more reliable knowledge.

The *Charvaka* School: Radical Materialist Doubt

At the opposite end of the spectrum from the spiritual certainties of the Upanishads and the Buddha, the *Charvaka* or *Lokayata* school of thought embraced radical materialist doubt. The *Charvakas* rejected the authority of the Vedas, the existence of an afterlife, and the concept of karma. For them, the only source of knowledge was direct sensory perception, and anything that could not be directly observed or experienced was to be doubted.

The *Charvaka* school was skeptical of metaphysical claims and dismissed the elaborate rituals and philosophical speculations of the Vedic tradition as meaningless. They argued that human life should be guided by pleasure and the pursuit of happiness in the here and now, rather than by concerns about an imagined afterlife or the accumulation of spiritual merit.

While the *Charvakas* were a minority school and their teachings were often criticized by other philosophers, their radical doubt served as a counterbalance to the spiritual certainties of the time. Their rejection of religious and philosophical dogma exemplifies the importance of doubt in questioning established norms and seeking alternative paths to understanding.

The Synthesis of Certainty and Doubt

The intellectual landscape of ancient India was characterized by a dynamic interplay between doubt and certainty. On one hand, the Upanishadic sages sought certainty in the realization of the ultimate truth, Brahman, through introspection and meditation. On the other hand, the Buddha's teachings on impermanence and non-self introduced a radical form of doubt that questioned the very nature of existence. The *Nyaya* philosophers developed a system of logic to resolve doubt and attain certainty through reason, while the *Charvakas* embraced doubt to challenge the religious and metaphysical certainties of their time.

What we see in these diverse schools of thought is that doubt was not viewed as an obstacle to knowledge but as a necessary stage in the search for truth. Whether it was the doubt that led the Buddha to enlightenment, the introspective doubt of the Upanishadic sages, or the logical doubt of the *Nyaya* philosophers, doubt served as a catalyst for deeper inquiry and more profound understanding.

In the search for meaning, doubt and certainty are not opposing forces but complementary aspects of the human experience. By embracing doubt, we open ourselves to new possibilities and avoid the trap of intellectual complacency. At the same time, the quest for certainty provides us with a sense of direction and purpose, guiding us in our exploration of life's most fundamental questions.

Chapter 5: The Limits of Knowledge: Epistemology and its Boundaries

The quest for knowledge is as old as human curiosity itself, and yet, despite millennia of intellectual exploration, the boundaries of what we can know remain a profound and often elusive subject. Epistemology, the branch of philosophy concerned with the nature, scope, and limits of knowledge, grapples with questions about what constitutes knowledge, how we acquire it, and how we can be certain of it. In this chapter, we will examine the limits of knowledge through various philosophical perspectives, exploring the challenges that arise when we push the boundaries of human understanding.

Epistemology: An Overview

Epistemology, derived from the Greek words *episteme* (knowledge) and *logos* (study), is the philosophical inquiry into the nature of knowledge. It seeks to answer fundamental questions such as: What is knowledge? How is it acquired? What are the limits of human understanding? Traditionally, epistemology has been concerned with issues such as the distinction between belief and knowledge, the sources of knowledge (such as perception, reason, and testimony), and the criteria for knowledge (such as justification and truth).

One of the key debates in epistemology is between *empiricism* and *rationalism*. Empiricists argue that knowledge comes primarily from sensory experience. According to this view, our understanding of the world is built upon observations and experiences, and anything that cannot be experienced or observed is outside the realm of knowledge. Rationalists, on the other hand, maintain that reason and logic are the primary sources of knowledge. They believe that certain truths can be known independently of sensory experience, through intellectual reasoning alone.

The limits of knowledge are deeply connected to these epistemological positions. Empiricists face the challenge of determining how much we can know based on our sensory experiences, which are inherently limited and fallible. Rationalists must grapple with the question of whether abstract reasoning can provide knowledge of the external world and whether it is possible to achieve certainty without empirical evidence.

The Limits of Sensory Knowledge

One of the fundamental questions in epistemology is the extent to which sensory experience can provide us with reliable knowledge. Sensory knowledge, derived from our senses—sight, hearing, touch, taste, and smell—forms the basis of our understanding of the external world. However, sensory experiences are often imperfect and can be deceptive. Optical illusions, auditory hallucinations, and other sensory distortions challenge the reliability of sensory knowledge.

The ancient Indian *Charvaka* school, with its materialist and empiricist perspective, emphasized the importance of sensory experience as the only valid source of knowledge. The Charvakas rejected metaphysical claims and spiritual doctrines that could not be directly perceived or experienced. While this view grounded knowledge in observable reality, it also faced limitations. For instance, the Charvakas' skepticism about the existence of an afterlife or the efficacy of rituals was based on the premise that only what can be directly observed is real. This stance, while rational, overlooks the possibility of truths that are not immediately perceptible but are still valid and significant.

Philosophers such as David Hume, a prominent empiricist, also grappled with the limits of sensory knowledge. Hume questioned the possibility of ever attaining certainty about causal relationships based on sensory experience alone. He argued that our belief in causality is a habit of thought rather than a logically necessary connection. According to Hume, while we observe patterns and regularities in the world, we can never truly know the causal mechanisms underlying them. This skepticism highlights a significant boundary in empirical knowledge—our sensory experiences can suggest patterns, but they cannot provide absolute certainty about the nature of causation.

The Challenge of Abstract Reasoning

In contrast to empiricism, rationalism posits that reason and logic are crucial to acquiring knowledge. Rationalists argue that certain truths can be known through intellectual reasoning alone, without reliance on sensory experience. For instance, mathematical truths and logical principles are often cited as examples of knowledge that is attained through reason rather than empirical observation.

However, the limits of abstract reasoning also present challenges. While logical and mathematical knowledge may be internally consistent, it does not always translate to empirical knowledge of the external world. For example, the principles of geometry and arithmetic are perfect in theory, but applying them to the real world often involves approximations and limitations. Additionally, rationalism must contend with the problem of how to justify the application of abstract principles to empirical reality. If reason alone is not grounded in sensory experience, how do we ensure that our rational deductions accurately reflect the external world?

Immanuel Kant, a key figure in epistemology, addressed the limits of both empirical and rationalist approaches in his work. Kant argued that while we can gain knowledge through sensory experience, our understanding is also shaped by the inherent structures of the mind. He introduced the concept of *categories*—innate conceptual frameworks that organize our sensory experiences. According to Kant, while we can have knowledge of phenomena (the world as it appears to us), the *noumenon* (the world as it is in itself) remains beyond our grasp. Kant's work underscores the limitations of both empirical and rationalist approaches, highlighting that our knowledge is constrained by both sensory data and the cognitive structures through which we interpret that data.

The Role of Testimony and Authority

Another significant source of knowledge is testimony—information provided by others. Testimonial knowledge is crucial in many areas of life, including historical understanding, scientific research, and everyday social interactions. However, relying on testimony introduces its own set of challenges and limitations. Testimony can be biased, inaccurate, or deceptive, raising questions about how we can ascertain the reliability of information provided by others.

In the context of religious and philosophical traditions, testimony often plays a central role. Sacred texts, spiritual teachers, and historical accounts are frequently relied upon to convey knowledge about the divine, moral principles, or the nature of existence. While such sources can provide valuable insights, they also require critical evaluation. The reliability of testimonial knowledge depends on the credibility of the sources, the consistency of their claims, and the alignment of their teachings with other forms of evidence.

The *Nyaya* school of ancient Indian philosophy, which we discussed in the previous chapter, developed an elaborate theory of knowledge that included testimony as one of its sources. The *Nyaya* philosophers recognized the importance of *pramana* (valid means of knowledge) and included testimony as one of the four primary sources, alongside perception, inference, and comparison. However, they also acknowledged the need for careful evaluation of testimonial sources to ensure their reliability.

The Limits of Knowledge and the Quest for Meaning

The limits of knowledge are not merely an academic concern but have profound implications for the search for meaning. Understanding the boundaries of what we can know influences how we approach existential questions, ethical dilemmas, and the nature of reality. The recognition of these limits can lead to a more nuanced and humble perspective on our place in the world.

The ancient Indian epics, such as the *Ramayana* and the *Mahabharata*, offer rich examples of how the limits of knowledge shape human experience. In the *Mahabharata*, the Bhagavad Gita addresses the tension between worldly knowledge and spiritual insight. Arjuna's dilemma on the battlefield reflects the limits of empirical knowledge and the need for deeper, intuitive understanding. Krishna's teachings guide Arjuna to see beyond the immediate and empirical, suggesting that true knowledge involves recognizing the limitations of sensory experience and embracing a higher, spiritual perspective.

Similarly, in the *Ramayana*, the character of Hanuman exemplifies the limits of human understanding and the transformative power of devotion. Hanuman's quest to find Sita and his subsequent feats demonstrate how faith and devotion can transcend the boundaries of conventional knowledge. His actions highlight the idea that certain truths and insights are accessible not through empirical observation or rational deduction alone but through a deeper connection with the divine.

The limits of knowledge are a fundamental aspect of epistemology and have profound implications for our understanding of the world. From the challenges of sensory experience and abstract reasoning to the role of testimony and authority, the boundaries of what we can know are shaped by a complex interplay of factors. The recognition of these limits invites us to approach knowledge with humility and curiosity, acknowledging both the power and the constraints of our intellectual pursuits.

In the search for meaning, the limits of knowledge remind us that certainty is often provisional and that the quest for understanding is ongoing. By exploring the boundaries of what we can know, we are better equipped to navigate the complexities of existence and to appreciate the richness of human experience. As we continue our journey through the landscape of doubt and certainty, we will find that the exploration of knowledge's limits is not a destination but an integral part of the search for meaning and understanding.

Chapter 6: The Quest for Meaning in a Chaotic World

In an era marked by unprecedented rapid change, technological advancements, and global interconnectedness, the quest for meaning has become both more complex and more urgent. Our modern world, characterized by its inherent chaos and uncertainty, challenges traditional frameworks for understanding existence and offers new perspectives on the search for purpose. In this chapter, we will explore how individuals and societies navigate the quest for meaning amidst the tumult of contemporary life. We will examine how existential philosophy, modern psychological insights, and cultural narratives address the search for meaning in a chaotic world.

The Nature of Chaos and Uncertainty

To understand the quest for meaning in a chaotic world, it is crucial to define what we mean by chaos and uncertainty. In a philosophical sense, chaos refers to the unpredictable and often disordered nature of reality, where events and outcomes are not always governed by discernible patterns. Uncertainty, on the other hand, pertains to the inability to predict or control outcomes due to the inherent unpredictability of the world.

Modern life is rife with examples of chaos and uncertainty. From political instability and economic upheavals to environmental crises and technological disruptions, individuals are frequently confronted with situations that defy easy explanation or control. The rapid pace of change often leaves people feeling disoriented and uncertain about their place in the world.

The concept of chaos is not new, and it has been explored in various philosophical and spiritual traditions. In Eastern philosophies such as Taoism, chaos is seen as an intrinsic part of the natural order, an aspect of the *Tao* (the Way) that governs the universe. The Taoist approach to chaos emphasizes harmony with the natural flow of life rather than attempting to impose order on it.

In Western philosophy, existentialists like Jean-Paul Sartre and Albert Camus grappled with the absurdity and inherent chaos of existence. Sartre's notion of *existential freedom* posits that individuals are condemned to be free, facing the chaos of an indifferent universe without inherent meaning. Camus, in his work *The Myth of Sisyphus*, describes life as fundamentally absurd, where the search for meaning in a chaotic world is a Sisyphean task—endless and inherently unresolvable.

Existential Philosophy: Finding Meaning Amidst Absurdity

Existential philosophy offers a framework for understanding and confronting the chaos and uncertainty of modern life.

Existentialists argue that meaning is not given but created, and individuals must confront the absurdity of existence to forge their own sense of purpose.

Sartre's philosophy of existentialism emphasizes the responsibility of individuals to create their own meaning in a world without inherent purpose. According to Sartre, humans are "condemned to be free," meaning that we must navigate the chaos of existence and make choices without the guidance of predetermined values or objectives. This freedom, while daunting, also offers the potential for authentic self-definition and personal significance.

Albert Camus, another prominent existentialist, approached the search for meaning from the perspective of the absurd. In *The Myth of Sisyphus*, Camus uses the story of Sisyphus, condemned to roll a boulder up a hill only for it to roll back down each time, as a metaphor for the human condition. Camus argues that even in the face of an absurd and meaningless universe, individuals can find fulfillment by embracing the struggle and absurdity of life. For Camus, the key to meaning lies in acknowledging the absurdity and continuing to engage with life passionately and defiantly.

Existential philosophy highlights that meaning is not an external reality to be discovered but a personal and subjective experience. In a chaotic world, individuals are challenged to confront their own existence, make choices, and create significance amidst uncertainty.

Psychological Perspectives on Meaning and Well-Being

Psychology offers valuable insights into how individuals find meaning and maintain well-being in the face of chaos. Modern psychological research has explored various aspects of meaning, including its impact on mental health, resilience, and overall life satisfaction.

Viktor Frankl, a psychiatrist and Holocaust survivor, developed a form of existential psychotherapy known as logotherapy. Frankl's experiences in concentration camps led him to conclude that the search for meaning is a fundamental human drive. In his seminal work, *Man's Search for Meaning*, Frankl argues that individuals can find purpose even in the most challenging circumstances by discovering a sense of meaning in their experiences. For Frankl, meaning can be found through work, relationships, and personal growth, and it is this search for purpose that can provide individuals with resilience and hope.

Positive psychology, a relatively recent field of study, also examines the role of meaning in well-being. Researchers such as Martin Seligman and Mihaly Csikszentmihalyi have investigated how factors like purpose, engagement, and flow contribute to a fulfilling life. Seligman's concept of *PERMA* (Positive Emotion, Engagement, Relationships, Meaning, and Accomplishment) emphasizes that meaning is a crucial component of overall well-being. According to positive psychology, meaning can be derived from various sources, including personal achievements, connections with others, and contributions to something larger than oneself.

The psychological approach to meaning underscores that individuals can actively shape their sense of purpose through their choices, relationships, and experiences. In a chaotic world, maintaining a sense of meaning can enhance resilience, foster mental health, and provide a sense of direction amidst uncertainty.

Cultural Narratives and Meaning-Making

Cultural narratives play a significant role in shaping how individuals and societies find meaning amidst chaos. Stories, myths, and traditions offer frameworks for understanding existence, providing context and coherence to individual and collective experiences.

The narratives found in literature, film, and popular culture often reflect and address the chaos of modern life. For example, contemporary dystopian fiction explores themes of societal collapse, existential dread, and the search for meaning in a fractured world. Works such as George Orwell's *1984* and Margaret Atwood's *The Handmaid's Tale* present visions of a world where traditional structures of meaning are upended, prompting readers to consider the implications for their own lives and societies.

In addition to fiction, cultural and religious traditions offer rich resources for meaning-making. Many religious traditions provide narratives that address existential questions and offer pathways to transcendence. For example, the Bhagavad Gita, a central text in Hindu philosophy, addresses the challenges of duty, righteousness, and the search for spiritual meaning in the midst of worldly chaos. The Gita's teachings encourage individuals to act according to their dharma (duty) while maintaining a sense of detachment from the fruits of their actions, thus navigating the chaos of life with purpose and equanimity.

Similarly, Buddhist teachings on impermanence and non-attachment offer insights into how to find meaning in a world marked by constant change. Buddhism encourages individuals to embrace the fluid nature of existence, to let go of clinging and attachment, and to cultivate mindfulness and compassion as sources of meaning and fulfillment.

Cultural narratives and religious traditions provide a sense of continuity and connection in a chaotic world. They offer frameworks for interpreting experiences, making sense of suffering, and finding purpose amidst the uncertainties of life.

The Personal Journey: Crafting Meaning in the Modern Age

In our rapidly changing world, individuals face the challenge of crafting their own sense of meaning in the face of external chaos and internal uncertainty. This personal journey involves reflecting on one's values, passions, and goals, and actively engaging in activities that align with one's sense of purpose.

The modern age presents unique opportunities and challenges for meaning-making. Technological advancements, globalization, and shifting social norms offer new avenues for exploration and self-expression. Social media, for example, can be a platform for connecting with like-minded individuals, pursuing creative projects, and engaging in causes that resonate with personal values.

However, it can also contribute to feelings of isolation, comparison, and superficiality.

Finding meaning in the modern age requires navigating the complexities of contemporary life while staying true to one's authentic self. It involves recognizing the transient nature of external conditions and focusing on internal sources of purpose and fulfillment. This journey may include exploring new interests, cultivating relationships, pursuing personal growth, and contributing to the well-being of others.

Ultimately, the quest for meaning in a chaotic world is a deeply personal endeavor. It involves acknowledging the challenges and uncertainties of life while seeking out sources of purpose and connection. By embracing the complexities of existence and actively shaping one's sense of meaning, individuals can navigate the chaos of the modern world with resilience and clarity.

The quest for meaning in a chaotic world is a multifaceted and ongoing journey. From existential philosophy and psychological insights to cultural narratives and personal exploration, the search for purpose involves confronting the challenges of uncertainty and disorder. Understanding the nature of chaos, embracing existential freedom, and drawing on cultural and psychological resources can help individuals navigate the complexities of modern life and find a sense of meaning and fulfillment.

As we continue our exploration of doubt, certainty, and meaning, we will delve deeper into the ways in which individuals and societies grapple with the fundamental questions of existence. The quest for meaning is not only a philosophical or intellectual pursuit but a deeply personal and transformative journey. In the face of a chaotic and unpredictable world, the search for purpose remains an essential and enduring aspect of the human experience.

Chapter 7: Faith and Reason: The Everlasting Struggle

The relationship between faith and reason has been a central theme in philosophical and theological discourse throughout history. These two modes of understanding—faith and reason—often seem to stand in tension with each other, each representing a different approach to comprehending truth and meaning. Faith, generally associated with belief in the unseen and the divine, relies on conviction and trust in spiritual or religious doctrines. Reason, on the other hand, emphasizes empirical evidence, logical consistency, and intellectual scrutiny. The interplay between these two realms raises profound questions about how we come to understand reality, make decisions, and find meaning in our lives. This chapter will explore the ongoing struggle between faith and reason, examining their respective roles and interactions, and how this dynamic has shaped human thought and culture.

The Nature of Faith

Faith is often defined as a strong belief in something that does not require empirical evidence or logical proof. In religious contexts, faith typically involves belief in the divine, spiritual truths, or sacred narratives. Faith is characterized by trust and conviction in the face of uncertainty and the unknown. It is not necessarily tied to empirical verification but is rooted in personal experience, spiritual insight, and communal tradition.

Historically, faith has been a central aspect of many religious traditions. In Christianity, for example, faith in God and the teachings of Jesus Christ are fundamental to the religious experience. The Apostle Paul, in his Epistle to the Hebrews, describes faith as "the assurance of things hoped for, the conviction of things not seen" (Hebrews 11:1). Similarly, in Islam, faith (*iman*) in Allah and His prophets is central to the practice of the religion. Faith provides a framework for understanding the world, guiding moral behavior, and offering solace and hope in the face of life's challenges.

Faith can offer a sense of purpose and meaning that transcends the material world. It can provide comfort, moral guidance, and a sense of belonging within a community. However, faith is also subject to scrutiny and criticism, especially when its claims conflict with scientific evidence or rational inquiry. This tension between faith and reason has been a recurring theme in philosophical and theological debates.

The Role of Reason

Reason, in contrast to faith, is grounded in the principles of logic, empirical evidence, and intellectual rigor. Reason involves critical thinking, analysis, and the use of evidence to draw conclusions. It is often associated with the scientific method, which relies on observation, experimentation, and the formulation of hypotheses to understand natural phenomena.

In the Enlightenment period, reason became a central focus in Western thought. Philosophers such as Immanuel Kant and David Hume championed reason as a means of achieving knowledge and understanding. Kant argued that reason is essential for understanding the world and making moral judgments. He posited that while empirical knowledge is limited to the realm of phenomena, reason provides a framework for understanding universal moral principles.

The rise of science and rationalism in the modern era has significantly influenced our understanding of reason. The scientific method has provided powerful tools for investigating the natural world and has led to numerous advancements in technology and medicine. However, reason alone does not address all aspects of human experience, particularly those related to meaning, value, and purpose. This limitation has led to ongoing discussions about the role of reason in understanding the full scope of human existence.

Historical Context: The Conflict and Reconciliation

The struggle between faith and reason has manifested in various historical contexts, often reflecting broader cultural and intellectual shifts. One of the most famous conflicts between faith and reason occurred during the Middle Ages and the Renaissance.

The medieval Scholastic tradition sought to reconcile faith with reason, aiming to demonstrate that religious beliefs could be supported by rational arguments. Figures such as Thomas Aquinas worked to harmonize Christian doctrine with Aristotelian philosophy. Aquinas's *Summa Theologica* is a landmark work that attempts to provide a rational foundation for faith, addressing questions about the existence of God, the nature of morality, and the relationship between reason and revelation.

The Enlightenment period, however, marked a shift towards reason as the primary means of understanding and explaining the world. Enlightenment thinkers, such as Voltaire and Diderot, critiqued religious dogma and championed reason, secularism, and scientific inquiry. This era witnessed significant advancements in science and philosophy, but also a growing tension between religious faith and rational skepticism.

The 19th and 20th centuries continued to explore the relationship between faith and reason, with various thinkers offering new perspectives. Friedrich Nietzsche famously declared the "death of God," challenging traditional religious beliefs and emphasizing the need for new sources of meaning in a secular world. In contrast, philosophers like William James and Søren Kierkegaard argued for the validity of faith as a legitimate and meaningful response to the limits of reason.

The Modern Dialogue: Integrating Faith and Reason

In contemporary philosophy and theology, the dialogue between faith and reason continues to evolve. Many scholars and thinkers seek to integrate these two perspectives, recognizing that both have valuable contributions to make in the quest for understanding.

One approach to reconciling faith and reason is the idea of *complementarity*. This perspective suggests that faith and reason address different aspects of human experience and can coexist without necessarily conflicting. For example, religious beliefs may provide answers to questions of ultimate purpose and meaning, while reason and science offer explanations about the natural world and practical matters.

Another approach is the concept of *critical realism*, which acknowledges that our understanding of reality is shaped by both empirical evidence and interpretive frameworks. This perspective recognizes that while scientific inquiry provides valuable insights, it is also informed by cultural, historical, and philosophical assumptions. Critical realism allows for a nuanced understanding of how faith and reason can interact and influence each other.

Interfaith dialogue and comparative religion studies also contribute to the conversation between faith and reason. By examining the diverse ways in which different religious traditions address questions of meaning and truth, scholars can explore commonalities and differences in how faith and reason are conceptualized and applied. This comparative approach can foster mutual understanding and respect among different belief systems.

Personal Reflections: Navigating the Struggle

On a personal level, navigating the struggle between faith and reason involves reflecting on one's own beliefs and values, and how they shape one's understanding of the world. Individuals may find themselves oscillating between faith and reason, seeking a balance that resonates with their own experiences and perspectives.

For some, faith provides a foundation for understanding life's purpose and moral values, while reason offers tools for navigating practical and intellectual challenges. For others, reason may serve as the primary means of understanding, with faith playing a more peripheral role. Each individual's journey is unique, and the integration of faith and reason can be a dynamic and evolving process.

In the context of contemporary issues such as ethical dilemmas, scientific advancements, and social justice, the interplay between faith and reason can offer valuable insights. For example, discussions about the ethical implications of emerging technologies, such as genetic engineering or artificial intelligence, often involve both rational analysis and ethical considerations rooted in religious or philosophical traditions. Similarly, debates about social justice and human rights can benefit from both empirical evidence and moral principles derived from various belief systems.

The struggle between faith and reason is a defining aspect of human intellectual and spiritual life. While these two modes of understanding often appear to be in conflict, they also offer complementary perspectives on the nature of reality, meaning, and purpose. The ongoing dialogue between faith and reason reflects the complexity of human experience and the quest for understanding in a multifaceted world.

As we continue our exploration of doubt, certainty, and meaning, the relationship between faith and reason will remain a central theme. By examining how these two realms interact and influence each other, we gain deeper insights into the nature of knowledge, belief, and the search for meaning. The quest for understanding is an enduring journey, marked by the interplay of faith, reason, and the ever-evolving landscape of human thought and experience.

Chapter 8: Mysticism and the Certainty of the Unseen

Mysticism, a tradition of seeking direct, experiential knowledge of the divine or ultimate reality, offers a unique perspective on the quest for meaning. Unlike conventional philosophical or theological approaches that rely on reason, empirical evidence, or doctrinal teachings, mysticism emphasizes personal, direct experience of the transcendent. This chapter will explore the role of mysticism in the search for meaning, examining how it addresses the certainty of the unseen and how mystical experiences challenge and complement other forms of knowing.

The Essence of Mysticism

Mysticism can be described as the pursuit of a direct, personal connection with the divine or ultimate reality. Mystics often report experiences of unity, transcendence, and profound insight that transcend ordinary perception and conceptual understanding. These experiences are characterized by a deep sense of connection with a greater whole, often accompanied by a sense of awe and wonder.

At its core, mysticism seeks to go beyond the limits of conventional knowledge and experience to grasp the ineffable and the transcendent. Mystics often describe their experiences in terms that are deeply personal and symbolic, recognizing that language and concepts are insufficient to fully capture the nature of the divine. As a result, mystical experiences are frequently characterized by paradox, such as the sense of unity in diversity or the presence of divine absence.

Mysticism is found in various religious and spiritual traditions, each offering its own understanding of the divine and its methods for attaining mystical experiences. In Christianity, mystics such as Teresa of Ávila and John of the Cross described profound experiences of divine union and the transformative power of mystical encounters. In Islam, Sufism represents the mystical dimension of the religion, with figures like Rumi and Al-Ghazali exploring themes of love, devotion, and spiritual realization. Hinduism and Buddhism also contain rich mystical traditions, including practices such as meditation, yoga, and devotion to deities, which aim to achieve direct experience of spiritual truths.

The Certainty of the Unseen

One of the defining features of mysticism is its focus on the unseen or the ineffable. Mystics often speak of experiencing realities that are beyond ordinary sensory perception or rational understanding. This aspect of mysticism challenges the conventional boundaries of knowledge and introduces the possibility of certainties that are not accessible through empirical or logical means.

The notion of certainty in mysticism is paradoxical. On one hand, mystical experiences are deeply personal and transformative, providing a sense of certainty and conviction to those who have them. On the other hand, these experiences are inherently subjective and may not be easily communicated or verified by others. This tension raises questions about the nature of certainty and how it relates to personal experience versus communal validation.

In Islamic mysticism, or Sufism, the concept of *ghayb* (the unseen) plays a crucial role. Sufis believe that the divine reality is hidden from ordinary perception and that true knowledge comes from direct, experiential contact with the divine. Sufi practices such as *dhikr* (remembrance of God) and *whirling* aim to transcend the material world and experience the divine presence. For Sufis, the certainty of the unseen is experienced as a deep, personal realization of God's presence and the interconnectedness of all existence.

Similarly, in Hinduism, the concept of *Brahman* (the ultimate reality) is considered to be beyond ordinary perception and understanding. Mystical experiences in Hinduism often involve direct encounters with this transcendent reality, leading to a profound sense of unity and enlightenment. Practices such as meditation, chanting, and devotion are seen as means to access this deeper reality and achieve certainty about the divine.

Mysticism and Rational Inquiry

The relationship between mysticism and rational inquiry is complex and often marked by tension. Mysticism, with its emphasis on direct, personal experience, can appear to stand in opposition to rationalism and empirical science, which prioritize evidence, logic, and systematic investigation.

However, mysticism and reason can also be seen as complementary. Mystical experiences often provide insights and perspectives that challenge conventional ways of thinking and open up new possibilities for understanding. For example, mystical encounters with the divine may lead to profound realizations about the nature of reality, consciousness, and the self, which can enrich and deepen philosophical and scientific inquiries.

Philosophers such as William James have recognized the value of mystical experiences in expanding our understanding of human consciousness and spirituality. In his work *The Varieties of Religious Experience*, James explores the diverse ways in which individuals experience the divine and argues for the significance of mystical experiences in understanding the broader scope of human experience. James acknowledges that while mystical experiences may not be subject to empirical verification, they nonetheless provide valuable insights into the nature of reality and the human condition.

In contemporary philosophy and psychology, there is growing interest in exploring the intersections between mysticism and scientific inquiry. Research into altered states of consciousness, such as those induced by meditation, psychedelics, or other spiritual practices, has revealed insights into the nature of perception, cognition, and well-being. These studies suggest that mystical experiences may have empirical correlates and that understanding these experiences can contribute to our knowledge of the mind and its capacities.

The Transformative Power of Mysticism

Mystical experiences often have a profound impact on individuals, leading to transformative changes in their lives and perspectives. These experiences can result in a deepened sense of purpose, enhanced empathy and compassion, and a greater appreciation for the interconnectedness of all life.

In many religious traditions, mystical encounters are seen as transformative moments of spiritual awakening. For example, in Christianity, the experience of divine union or communion can lead to a renewed sense of faith, devotion, and moral commitment. Mystical experiences often inspire individuals to live in alignment with their spiritual values and to seek a deeper connection with others.

Similarly, in Hinduism and Buddhism, mystical experiences can lead to a heightened sense of self-realization and liberation from the cycle of suffering. Practices such as meditation and devotion are aimed at achieving states of consciousness that transcend the ego and reveal the true nature of reality. The transformative effects of these experiences can manifest in various ways, including increased inner peace, resilience, and a profound sense of connection with the universe.

The transformative power of mysticism extends beyond individual experiences to influence broader cultural and societal movements. Mystical traditions often emphasize values such as compassion, non-violence, and interconnectedness, which can inspire social and humanitarian efforts. Mystics have historically played a role in advocating for social justice, peace, and ethical living, drawing on their experiences of transcendent unity and divine love.

Mysticism and the Search for Meaning

Mysticism offers a distinctive approach to the search for meaning by focusing on direct, personal encounters with the divine or ultimate reality. These experiences provide individuals with a sense of certainty and insight that transcends conventional modes of knowing. While mystical experiences may not be easily communicated or validated by others, they hold profound significance for those who experience them.

The search for meaning through mysticism often involves exploring the depths of consciousness, embracing the mysteries of existence, and seeking connection with a transcendent reality. Mystical experiences challenge conventional boundaries of knowledge and invite individuals to explore the unseen dimensions of their own being and the world around them.

In the broader context of the quest for meaning, mysticism offers a valuable perspective on the nature of reality, consciousness, and the divine. By engaging with the mysteries of existence and embracing the uncertainty of the unseen, mystics provide insights that enrich and expand our understanding of the human experience.

Mysticism and the certainty of the unseen offer a unique and profound dimension to the search for meaning. Through direct, personal experiences of the divine or ultimate reality, mystics challenge conventional modes of understanding and offer insights that transcend empirical and rational inquiry. The transformative power of mystical experiences, along with their impact on individual and societal values, highlights the significance of mysticism in the broader quest for meaning.

As we continue our exploration of doubt, certainty, and meaning, the role of mysticism provides a rich and multifaceted perspective on the nature of reality and the divine. Mysticism invites us to embrace the mysteries of existence, seek connection with the transcendent, and find meaning in the ever-present uncertainty of the unseen.

Chapter 9: The Ethical Dilemmas of Certainty and Doubt

The concepts of certainty and doubt are not merely abstract philosophical ideas; they have profound implications for how we navigate ethical dilemmas in our daily lives. Our beliefs about what is certain or uncertain shape our moral judgments, influence our decision-making processes, and impact our interactions with others. This chapter explores how certainty and doubt intersect with ethical issues, examining the moral challenges that arise from these concepts and how they inform our understanding of right and wrong.

The Moral Implications of Certainty

Certainty in ethical decision-making often provides a strong sense of confidence and direction. When individuals are certain about their moral beliefs or values, they are typically more resolute in their decisions and actions. This sense of certainty can be beneficial in providing a clear framework for ethical behavior, offering guidance in complex situations, and fostering moral consistency.

However, certainty can also lead to ethical rigidity and dogmatism. When individuals hold their moral beliefs with absolute certainty, they may become intolerant of differing viewpoints and less open to dialogue or compromise. This rigidity can contribute to moral conflicts and exacerbate divisions within societies. For example, certain ideological or religious certainties have historically led to conflicts, discrimination, and violence against those with differing beliefs or practices.

Ethical certainty can also pose risks when it leads to a lack of critical reflection. If individuals are too confident in their moral judgments, they may overlook important nuances, fail to consider alternative perspectives, or ignore evidence that challenges their beliefs. This can result in ethical blind spots and misguided actions that have negative consequences for others.

In some cases, certainty about moral principles can be a force for good, driving individuals and groups to stand up for justice, human rights, and ethical reform. For example, the unwavering commitment of civil rights activists to the principle of equality played a crucial role in advancing social justice. However, even in such cases, it is important to balance certainty with humility and openness to ensure that moral convictions are informed by ongoing reflection and dialogue.

The Role of Doubt in Ethical Reflection

Doubt, in contrast to certainty, introduces a level of uncertainty and questioning into ethical decision-making. While doubt can be uncomfortable and disorienting, it also serves as a valuable tool for moral reflection and growth. When individuals encounter doubt, they are prompted to critically examine their beliefs, consider alternative viewpoints, and engage in deeper ethical reasoning.

Doubt can lead to greater ethical sensitivity and empathy. By acknowledging the limitations of one's own perspective and being open to the experiences and viewpoints of others, individuals can develop a more nuanced understanding of ethical issues. This process of reflective doubt can foster moral humility and a willingness to revise one's beliefs in light of new evidence or insights.

In ethical dilemmas, doubt can prompt individuals to explore the complexities of moral decision-making and seek solutions that consider the interests and well-being of all affected parties. For example, in situations where conflicting moral principles are at play, doubt can lead individuals to engage in deliberative processes that weigh the potential consequences of different courses of action and strive for ethical outcomes that balance competing values.

However, excessive doubt can also paralyze decision-making and lead to ethical indecision. When individuals are overwhelmed by uncertainty, they may struggle to make choices or take action, resulting in moral inaction or avoidance of difficult issues. Finding a balance between healthy skepticism and decisive action is crucial for effective ethical decision-making.

Ethical Dilemmas in Practice: Case Studies

To illustrate the ethical dilemmas arising from certainty and doubt, we can examine several case studies that highlight the complexities of moral decision-making.

1. **Medical Ethics and Certainty**

    o   **Case Study:** A physician faces a dilemma regarding the administration of a life-saving treatment to a terminally ill patient. The treatment has a high probability of extending the patient's life but also carries significant risks and potential side effects. The physician is certain about the medical benefits of the treatment but faces uncertainty about the patient's wishes and the overall quality of life.

    o   **Analysis:** The physician's certainty about the treatment's efficacy may guide their recommendation, but the uncertainty surrounding the patient's preferences and quality of life requires careful consideration. Ethical decision-making in this context involves balancing medical certainty with respect for patient autonomy and well-being.

2. **Business Ethics and Doubt**

- o **Case Study:** A business executive discovers that their company's product has a defect that could potentially harm consumers. The executive is uncertain about the extent of the harm and the best course of action. They face pressure from stakeholders to minimize the impact on the company's reputation and financial performance.

- o **Analysis:** The executive's doubt about the implications of the defect and the potential consequences of disclosure requires a thoughtful ethical response. Balancing transparency, consumer safety, and corporate responsibility involves navigating the uncertainties of potential harm while upholding ethical standards.

3. **Social Justice and Moral Certainty**

   - o **Case Study:** An activist is committed to advocating for social justice and equality. They are certain about the moral imperative to address systemic injustices but face doubt about the most effective strategies and tactics for achieving meaningful change.

   - o **Analysis:** The activist's certainty about the need for justice drives their commitment, but the uncertainties surrounding the effectiveness of different approaches require strategic reflection and adaptability. Ethical decision-making in this context involves aligning moral convictions with practical considerations and ongoing evaluation.

The Balance Between Certainty and Doubt

Navigating ethical dilemmas requires finding a balance between certainty and doubt. Certainty can provide clarity and direction, while doubt can encourage critical reflection and openness to new perspectives. Striking this balance involves recognizing the strengths and limitations of both approaches and integrating them into ethical decision-making processes.

1. **Embracing Ethical Pluralism:** Ethical pluralism acknowledges that multiple moral perspectives and values can coexist. By embracing this approach, individuals can navigate the complexities of ethical dilemmas with a recognition of diverse viewpoints and the potential for ethical ambiguity. This perspective encourages dialogue, empathy, and a willingness to find common ground.

2. **Cultivating Moral Humility:** Moral humility involves recognizing the limits of one's own certainty and being open to the possibility of being wrong or incomplete in one's understanding. By cultivating humility, individuals can approach ethical dilemmas with greater sensitivity and a readiness to revise their beliefs in light of new evidence or perspectives.

3. **Fostering Reflective Practice:** Reflective practice involves regularly examining one's ethical beliefs and decisions, considering the implications of certainty

and doubt, and seeking feedback from others. This practice can enhance ethical decision-making by promoting ongoing reflection, learning, and growth.

The ethical dilemmas of certainty and doubt highlight the complex interplay between confidence and questioning in moral decision-making. While certainty can provide direction and conviction, it can also lead to rigidity and blind spots. Doubt, on the other hand, encourages critical reflection and empathy but may result in indecision and inaction.

Navigating these dilemmas involves balancing the strengths and limitations of both certainty and doubt, embracing ethical pluralism, cultivating moral humility, and fostering reflective practice. By integrating these approaches, individuals can address ethical challenges with greater sensitivity, openness, and responsibility, ultimately contributing to more thoughtful and compassionate moral decision-making. As we continue our exploration of doubt, certainty, and meaning, the ethical dimensions of these concepts remain central to understanding how we navigate the complexities of human experience and uphold our values in a diverse and uncertain world.

Chapter 10: Freedom in Doubt: The Liberation of Uncertainty

Uncertainty is often perceived as a source of anxiety and hesitation, challenging our desire for clear answers and firm convictions. However, it can also be a powerful catalyst for freedom and liberation. By embracing uncertainty, individuals can transcend rigid constraints, explore new possibilities, and cultivate a deeper sense of personal and intellectual freedom. This chapter explores how doubt and uncertainty can lead to liberation, examining the ways in which they offer opportunities for growth, creativity, and self-discovery.

The Constraints of Certainty

Certainty, while providing a sense of security and direction, can also impose limitations on our thinking and behavior. When we are certain about our beliefs, values, or knowledge, we may become constrained by fixed perspectives and rigid frameworks. Certainty can lead to intellectual and emotional stagnation, limiting our ability to question, explore, and adapt.

In the realm of personal identity, certainty about one's self-concept can inhibit growth and change. For example, a fixed sense of identity may prevent individuals from exploring new aspects of themselves or adapting to evolving circumstances. This rigidity can lead to a lack of fulfillment and an inability to fully engage with the complexities of life.

Similarly, in the realm of knowledge and understanding, certainty can lead to intellectual dogmatism. When individuals are certain about their knowledge, they may become resistant to new information, perspectives, or evidence. This can hinder intellectual progress and limit the ability to engage with diverse viewpoints and emerging insights.

Embracing Uncertainty as a Path to Freedom

Uncertainty, on the other hand, offers the potential for liberation by challenging established boundaries and opening up new possibilities. By embracing uncertainty, individuals can break free from rigid constraints and explore a wider range of experiences, ideas, and perspectives.

1. **Openness to New Possibilities:** Uncertainty allows individuals to remain open to new possibilities and opportunities. When we acknowledge that our knowledge and understanding are provisional and subject to change, we become more receptive to novel ideas and experiences. This openness can lead to personal growth, intellectual innovation, and creative exploration.

   o **Example:** Consider the process of artistic creation. Artists often embrace uncertainty in their work, allowing for experimentation, spontaneity, and unexpected outcomes. This embrace of uncertainty can lead to the development of new styles, techniques, and expressions that might not have emerged from a more rigid approach.

2. **Flexibility and Adaptability:** Uncertainty fosters flexibility and adaptability by encouraging individuals to navigate complex and evolving situations with resilience and resourcefulness. When we are willing to adapt to changing circumstances and revise our beliefs in light of new information, we enhance our ability to respond effectively to challenges and opportunities.

   o **Example:** In the business world, companies that embrace uncertainty and remain adaptable to market changes are often better positioned for long-term success. By being open to evolving trends and consumer preferences, businesses can innovate and remain competitive in dynamic environments.

3. **Personal Growth and Self-Discovery:** Embracing uncertainty can facilitate personal growth and self-discovery by encouraging individuals to explore their own values, beliefs, and potentials. When we are willing to question and examine our assumptions, we open ourselves to deeper self-understanding and the possibility of transformative change.

   o **Example:** Individuals who embark on journeys of self-discovery, such as through travel, education, or introspection, often find that embracing uncertainty leads to profound insights about themselves and their place in the world. This process of exploration can result in a richer, more nuanced understanding of one's identity and purpose.

The Liberation of Uncertainty in Practice

The liberation of uncertainty involves actively engaging with the opportunities that doubt and ambiguity present. This engagement requires a willingness to embrace risk, challenge established norms, and explore new avenues for growth and creativity.

1. **Cultivating a Growth Mindset:** A growth mindset involves viewing challenges and uncertainties as opportunities for learning and development. By

adopting this mindset, individuals can approach difficulties with curiosity and resilience, seeing them as chances to expand their capabilities and understanding.

- **Example:** In education, a growth mindset encourages students to view their struggles and failures as part of the learning process. This approach fosters a positive attitude towards uncertainty and challenges, leading to greater perseverance and achievement.

2. **Exploring Alternative Perspectives:** Engaging with uncertainty can involve exploring diverse perspectives and ideas. By actively seeking out and considering viewpoints different from our own, we can gain a more comprehensive understanding of complex issues and enrich our own thinking.

- **Example:** Interdisciplinary research often involves integrating insights from different fields of study to address complex problems. This approach embraces uncertainty and diversity of thought, leading to innovative solutions and new ways of understanding.

3. **Practicing Mindfulness and Reflection:** Mindfulness and reflective practices can help individuals navigate uncertainty with greater ease and clarity. By cultivating awareness of the present moment and examining our thoughts and emotions, we can develop a more balanced and resilient approach to dealing with ambiguity.

- o **Example:** Mindfulness meditation can help individuals manage stress and anxiety related to uncertainty by fostering a sense of acceptance and presence. This practice can enhance emotional well-being and provide a foundation for navigating complex situations with greater composure.

The Ethical Dimension of Freedom in Uncertainty

The liberation of uncertainty also has ethical implications, particularly in relation to personal and collective responsibility. Embracing uncertainty requires a commitment to ethical reflection and consideration of the impact of our actions on others.

1. **Ethical Responsibility:** Navigating uncertainty involves recognizing our responsibility to act ethically and consider the potential consequences of our decisions. By embracing uncertainty, we can approach ethical dilemmas with greater humility and a willingness to engage in thoughtful deliberation.

   - o **Example:** In environmental ethics, uncertainty about the long-term effects of human activities on the planet requires a commitment to responsible stewardship and precautionary measures. Embracing uncertainty can lead to more sustainable practices and a greater focus on the well-being of future generations.

2. **Fostering Inclusivity and Respect:** Embracing uncertainty can lead to a more inclusive and respectful approach to diverse viewpoints and experiences. By acknowledging the limitations of our own perspectives and being open to the perspectives of others, we can foster greater understanding and collaboration.

   - **Example:** In social and political contexts, embracing uncertainty can lead to more inclusive policies and practices that consider the needs and voices of marginalized communities. This approach promotes greater equity and respect for diversity.

The liberation of uncertainty offers a powerful pathway to personal and intellectual freedom. By embracing the challenges and opportunities presented by doubt and ambiguity, individuals can transcend rigid constraints, explore new possibilities, and cultivate a deeper sense of self-discovery and creativity. The balance between certainty and uncertainty is essential for navigating the complexities of life, and embracing uncertainty can lead to a more open, adaptable, and ethically responsible approach to decision-making and personal growth.

As we continue to explore the themes of doubt, certainty, and meaning, the concept of freedom in uncertainty invites us to reconsider our relationship with ambiguity and embrace the transformative potential it offers. By fostering openness, adaptability, and ethical responsibility, we can navigate the uncertainties of life with greater resilience and creativity, ultimately enriching our understanding of ourselves and the world around us.

Chapter 11: The Role of Doubt in Political and Social Thought

Doubt plays a critical role in shaping political and social thought, influencing both individual perspectives and collective actions. While certainty often drives ideological commitments and policy decisions, doubt introduces a level of scrutiny and questioning that can lead to more nuanced understandings and progressive changes. This chapter explores how doubt functions in political and social contexts, examining its impact on governance, activism, and public discourse.

The Dynamics of Certainty and Doubt in Political Ideologies

Political ideologies often thrive on certainty, providing individuals and groups with clear principles and frameworks for understanding the world and guiding their actions. Certainty can foster unity and cohesion within political movements, but it can also lead to dogmatism and exclusion of dissenting viewpoints. Doubt, in contrast, encourages critical examination and openness to alternative perspectives, which can lead to more balanced and reflective political thought.

1. **Ideological Rigidity and Flexibility:** Political ideologies that embrace certainty may become rigid and resistant to change, limiting their ability to adapt to evolving circumstances or new information. This rigidity can result in policies and practices that fail to address emerging issues or adequately represent diverse interests.

   o **Example:** The ideological rigidity of certain political regimes can lead to authoritarianism and suppression of dissent. When political leaders are certain of their ideology and dismiss dissenting views, it can stifle democratic processes and restrict individual freedoms. In contrast, political systems that embrace doubt and encourage debate may be more responsive to changing needs and perspectives.

2. **The Role of Doubt in Policy Reform:** Doubt can drive policy reform by prompting critical examination of existing practices and the exploration of alternative approaches. When policymakers and citizens question the effectiveness and fairness of current policies, they can identify areas for improvement and advocate for more equitable solutions.

   o **Example:** Social movements advocating for criminal justice reform often challenge the certainty surrounding traditional punitive approaches. By questioning the effectiveness of current practices and highlighting issues of racial and socioeconomic disparity, these movements drive efforts to explore alternative models of justice and rehabilitation.

Doubt and Activism: The Pursuit of Social Change

Activism often thrives on the ability to question established norms and advocate for transformative change. Doubt can fuel social movements by encouraging activists to challenge the status quo, seek out new ideas, and address systemic injustices. The role of doubt in activism is crucial for driving progress and achieving social change.

1. **Challenging the Status Quo:** Activists frequently embrace doubt to question prevailing social norms and advocate for change. This questioning of

established practices and beliefs can lead to the identification of injustices and the development of innovative solutions.

- o **Example:** The civil rights movement in the United States questioned the certainty of racial segregation and discrimination. Activists used doubt to challenge the legitimacy of racist laws and practices, ultimately leading to significant legal and social reforms aimed at achieving greater equality.

2. **Fostering Inclusivity and Dialogue:** Doubt in activism can promote inclusivity and dialogue by encouraging the exploration of diverse perspectives and experiences. Activists who are open to questioning their own assumptions and engaging with different viewpoints can build more inclusive movements and address a wider range of issues.

- o **Example:** The feminist movement has evolved through various waves, each characterized by doubt and questioning of previous assumptions about gender roles and equality. This process of critical reflection and dialogue has led to more nuanced understandings of gender and the inclusion of diverse voices within the movement.

The Influence of Doubt on Public Discourse

Public discourse benefits from the presence of doubt, as it encourages critical engagement with ideas and fosters a more dynamic and inclusive exchange of views. Doubt can lead to more informed and reflective discussions, contributing to the health of democratic processes and the advancement of social knowledge.

1. **Encouraging Critical Thinking:** Doubt promotes critical thinking by challenging individuals to question and evaluate the information and arguments presented to them. This critical engagement is essential for informed decision-making and the development of well-reasoned opinions.

   o **Example:** In democratic societies, public debates and discussions often involve a range of perspectives and opinions. The presence of doubt and critical questioning helps to ensure that policies and decisions are subject to rigorous scrutiny and that diverse viewpoints are considered.

2. **Addressing Misinformation and Bias:** Doubt can also play a role in addressing misinformation and bias by encouraging individuals to verify information and consider alternative sources. A skeptical approach to information can help prevent the spread of falsehoods and promote a more accurate understanding of social and political issues.

   o **Example:** In the era of digital media, the prevalence of misinformation and fake news has raised concerns about the quality of public discourse. Encouraging doubt and critical evaluation of information sources can help individuals navigate this complex landscape and make more informed judgments.

The Ethical Dimensions of Doubt in Political and Social Contexts

The role of doubt in political and social thought also involves ethical considerations, particularly in relation to responsibility, integrity, and respect for differing viewpoints.

1. **Ethical Responsibility in Advocacy:** Activists and policymakers who embrace doubt must navigate the ethical implications of their actions and decisions. This involves considering the potential impact of their efforts on different communities and ensuring that their actions align with ethical principles of fairness and justice.

   o **Example:** Environmental activists who question the impact of industrial practices must balance their advocacy with considerations of economic and social consequences. Ethical responsibility involves seeking solutions that address environmental concerns while also considering the needs and livelihoods of affected communities.

2. **Respect for Diverse Perspectives:** Embracing doubt in public discourse requires respect for diverse perspectives and a commitment to constructive

dialogue. Engaging with differing viewpoints and addressing potential biases is essential for fostering a more inclusive and equitable public discourse.

- o **Example:** Political debates and discussions benefit from respectful engagement with opposing viewpoints. By approaching disagreements with an open mind and a willingness to understand differing perspectives, individuals can contribute to more productive and meaningful exchanges.

The role of doubt in political and social thought is multifaceted, influencing how individuals and societies navigate ideologies, activism, and public discourse. While certainty can provide direction and cohesion, doubt introduces a level of scrutiny and questioning that can lead to more nuanced understandings and transformative change.

Embracing doubt in political and social contexts involves recognizing the limitations of established norms, challenging prevailing assumptions, and fostering open and inclusive dialogue. By integrating doubt into our approach to governance, activism, and public discourse, we can contribute to more reflective, equitable, and progressive societies.

As we continue to explore the themes of doubt, certainty, and meaning, the role of doubt in shaping political and social thought highlights the importance of critical engagement, ethical responsibility, and respect for diverse perspectives. By navigating the complexities of political and social issues with an openness to uncertainty, we can advance our understanding and work towards a more just and inclusive world.

Chapter 12: Technology, Knowledge, and the New Age of Uncertainty

The advent of technology has profoundly transformed the way we acquire, process, and understand knowledge, ushering in a new era of uncertainty. As digital technologies reshape our world, they also challenge traditional notions of certainty and knowledge, presenting both opportunities and complexities. This chapter explores how technology influences our understanding of uncertainty, examining its impact on knowledge, information, and societal dynamics.

The Evolution of Knowledge in the Digital Age

The digital revolution has dramatically altered the landscape of knowledge, from the way information is accessed to the speed at which it is disseminated. The transition from print to digital media has introduced new forms of uncertainty and challenges, reshaping our approach to knowledge and information.

1. **Information Overload and Fragmentation:** The internet and digital technologies have led to an unprecedented increase in the volume of available information. While this abundance offers opportunities for learning and discovery, it also creates challenges related to information overload and fragmentation. Navigating this vast sea of information requires new strategies for filtering, evaluating, and synthesizing knowledge.

   o **Example:** Social media platforms, with their rapid dissemination of news and opinions, contribute to the fragmentation of information. Users are often exposed to conflicting reports and perspectives, making it challenging to discern reliable sources and form coherent understandings of current events.

2. **The Role of Algorithms and Personalization:**
   Algorithms and data-driven technologies play a
   significant role in shaping the information we
   encounter. Personalized content, driven by
   algorithms, can create echo chambers and reinforce
   existing beliefs, potentially limiting exposure to
   diverse viewpoints and contributing to a fragmented
   understanding of complex issues.

   o **Example:** Recommendation algorithms on
     streaming services and social media
     platforms often suggest content based on
     users' previous interactions. This
     personalized approach can lead to a
     narrowing of perspectives, as users are
     primarily exposed to information that aligns
     with their existing preferences and beliefs.

Uncertainty and the Changing Nature of Expertise

The rapid evolution of technology has also impacted the
concept of expertise and the way knowledge is validated.
Traditional notions of expertise, based on established
credentials and authoritative sources, are increasingly
challenged by the dynamic and decentralized nature of
digital information.

1. **Decentralization of Expertise:** Digital platforms
   enable the proliferation of diverse voices and
   perspectives, allowing individuals without formal
   expertise to contribute to public discourse and
   knowledge creation. While this democratization of
   knowledge can foster innovation and inclusivity, it

also raises questions about the credibility and reliability of information sources.

- o **Example:** Online forums and social media have given rise to a wide range of voices on topics ranging from health to politics. While this diversity of input can be valuable, it also requires critical evaluation of sources and an understanding of the limitations of informal expertise.

2. **The Challenge of Misinformation:** The ease of publishing and sharing information online has led to the spread of misinformation and disinformation. As technology enables the rapid dissemination of false or misleading content, distinguishing between accurate and inaccurate information becomes increasingly challenging.

- o **Example:** The spread of conspiracy theories and fake news on social media platforms highlights the difficulties of discerning credible information in the digital age. Efforts to combat misinformation involve both technological solutions, such as fact-checking algorithms, and educational initiatives to promote media literacy.

Technology and the Dynamics of Uncertainty

Technology not only influences our understanding of knowledge but also affects how we experience and respond to uncertainty. The interaction between technology and uncertainty manifests in various ways, from the management of risk to the adaptation of societal systems.

1. **Managing Risk and Uncertainty:** Technological advancements offer tools and methods for managing and mitigating uncertainty. Predictive algorithms, data analytics, and risk assessment technologies provide valuable insights and forecasts, helping individuals and organizations navigate uncertainty more effectively.

   o **Example:** In the field of finance, predictive models and risk management tools help investors and institutions make informed decisions amidst market uncertainties. These technologies can analyze large datasets to identify trends and potential risks, aiding in strategic planning and decision-making.

2. **The Impact on Societal Systems:** Technology also influences societal systems, from healthcare to governance. The integration of digital technologies into various sectors can lead to more efficient processes and improved outcomes, but it also introduces new forms of uncertainty and complexity.

   o **Example:** The use of artificial intelligence (AI) in healthcare has the potential to enhance diagnostic accuracy and treatment options. However, it also raises ethical and practical concerns, such as data privacy and the potential for algorithmic biases, which need to be addressed as technology continues to evolve.

The Ethical and Philosophical Dimensions of Technological Uncertainty

The intersection of technology and uncertainty raises important ethical and philosophical questions. As technology continues to advance, it is crucial to consider the implications for individuals, societies, and the broader ethical landscape.

1. **Ethical Considerations in Technology Development:** The development and deployment of technology involve ethical considerations related to privacy, security, and fairness. Ensuring that technological innovations align with ethical principles and address potential risks is essential for responsible progress.

   o **Example:** The implementation of facial recognition technology raises concerns about privacy and surveillance. Ethical considerations involve balancing the benefits of enhanced security with the potential for misuse and the impact on individual freedoms.

2. **Philosophical Reflections on Knowledge and Truth:** The digital age challenges traditional notions of knowledge and truth, prompting philosophical reflections on the nature of reality, certainty, and belief. As technology reshapes our understanding of these concepts, it is important to explore their

implications for our epistemological and ontological frameworks.

- **Example:** The concept of "post-truth," where emotional appeal and personal belief outweigh objective facts, highlights the philosophical challenges of defining and understanding truth in the digital age. This shift prompts reflections on the nature of truth and the role of technology in shaping our perceptions.

Navigating the Future: Embracing Uncertainty in the Digital Age

As we move forward in an increasingly digital world, embracing uncertainty becomes a key strategy for navigating the complexities of technology and knowledge. By recognizing the opportunities and challenges presented by technological advancements, we can develop more adaptive and resilient approaches to managing uncertainty.

1. **Cultivating Digital Literacy:** Enhancing digital literacy and critical thinking skills is essential for navigating the complexities of the digital age. By developing the ability to critically evaluate information, understand the limitations of technology, and engage with diverse perspectives, individuals can better manage uncertainty and make informed decisions.

   - **Example:** Educational initiatives focused on digital literacy and media education can help individuals develop skills to discern reliable information, understand algorithmic influences, and navigate the digital landscape with greater awareness and responsibility.

2. **Fostering Responsible Innovation:** Encouraging responsible innovation involves considering the ethical implications of technological advancements and ensuring that they align with societal values and goals. By integrating ethical considerations into the development and deployment of technology, we can address potential risks and promote positive outcomes.

   o **Example:** Collaborative efforts between technologists, ethicists, and policymakers can lead to the creation of guidelines and standards for responsible technology use. This approach helps ensure that technological innovations contribute to the common good while mitigating potential negative impacts.

The new age of uncertainty, driven by technological advancements, presents both challenges and opportunities for understanding and managing knowledge. Technology reshapes our perceptions of certainty and knowledge, introducing complexities that require thoughtful consideration and adaptive strategies.

By embracing uncertainty and recognizing the impact of technology on knowledge and societal dynamics, we can navigate the digital age with greater resilience and insight. Cultivating digital literacy, fostering responsible innovation, and engaging in philosophical reflections on knowledge and truth are essential for navigating the complexities of technology and uncertainty.

As we continue our exploration of doubt, certainty, and meaning, the role of technology in shaping our understanding of these concepts highlights the need for a balanced and reflective approach to managing knowledge and navigating the uncertainties of the digital age. Through critical engagement and ethical consideration, we can navigate the evolving landscape of technology with greater awareness and responsibility, ultimately enriching our understanding of ourselves and the world around us.

Chapter 13: Spirituality in the Age of Doubt

In an era marked by rapid technological advancement and a pervasive sense of uncertainty, spirituality provides a vital counterbalance to the complexities of modern life. The search for meaning and transcendence remains a fundamental human quest, even as traditional structures of belief and practice face scrutiny and transformation. This chapter explores how spirituality adapts and endures in the age of doubt, examining its evolving role in providing guidance, solace, and purpose amidst contemporary challenges.

The Nature of Spirituality in Modern Times

Spirituality encompasses a wide range of beliefs, practices, and experiences related to the search for meaning, connection, and transcendence. In the age of doubt, spirituality evolves as individuals grapple with the impact of scientific advancements, societal changes, and existential questions.

1. **Reconceiving Spirituality:** As traditional religious institutions and doctrines face increasing skepticism, many individuals turn to more personalized and eclectic forms of spirituality. This shift reflects a growing desire for spiritual practices that resonate with personal experiences and values, rather than conforming to established norms.

   o **Example:** The rise of mindfulness practices, meditation, and holistic well-being approaches represents a shift towards spirituality that integrates psychological, physical, and emotional dimensions. These practices offer a way to cultivate inner peace and connection without necessarily adhering to specific religious traditions.

2. **Spirituality and Secularism:** The intersection of spirituality and secularism reflects a broader trend

towards integrating spiritual practices into secular lifestyles. Many people seek spiritual fulfillment outside traditional religious frameworks, blending elements of various spiritual and philosophical traditions to create personalized paths to meaning.

- **Example:** The concept of "spiritual but not religious" (SBNR) reflects a growing movement of individuals who identify with spiritual practices and beliefs but do not align with organized religions. This approach allows for a more flexible and individualized exploration of spirituality.

The Role of Spirituality in Addressing Uncertainty

Spirituality can play a crucial role in addressing the uncertainties of modern life by providing frameworks for understanding existential questions, coping with challenges, and finding a sense of purpose and connection.

1. **Navigating Existential Questions:** Spirituality offers tools for grappling with fundamental existential questions, such as the nature of existence, purpose, and the meaning of life. By providing narratives and practices that address these questions, spirituality can offer comfort and direction amidst uncertainty.

   - **Example:** Contemplative practices, such as meditation and prayer, can provide individuals with a sense of inner clarity and perspective. These practices help individuals explore and reflect on their sense of purpose and place in the world.

2. **Coping with Life's Challenges:** Spirituality can offer resources for managing life's challenges and uncertainties, such as illness, loss, and personal crises. Spiritual beliefs and practices can provide emotional support, resilience, and a sense of hope during difficult times.

   o **Example:** Spiritual support groups and communities often provide a space for individuals to share their experiences, seek guidance, and find solidarity. These groups can offer a sense of belonging and support, helping individuals navigate challenging circumstances with a sense of purpose and connection.

Spiritual Practices in a Technological Age

The integration of technology into spiritual practices reflects both the opportunities and challenges of modern life. Technology can enhance access to spiritual resources and communities, but it also raises questions about the authenticity and impact of digital spirituality.

1. **Digital Spirituality and Community:** Technology facilitates the creation of virtual spiritual communities and the dissemination of spiritual resources. Online platforms and apps provide access to spiritual practices, teachings, and support, making spirituality more accessible to a global audience.

- o **Example:** Meditation and mindfulness apps offer guided practices and resources to users, allowing them to integrate spiritual practices into their daily lives. Virtual spiritual communities and online forums provide spaces for individuals to connect with others who share similar spiritual interests.

2. **Challenges of Digital Spirituality:** While technology offers opportunities for spiritual engagement, it also raises concerns about the impact of digital interactions on spiritual experiences. The virtual nature of online spirituality may lack the depth and personal connection of in-person practices and communities.

   - o **Example:** Online spiritual practices, such as virtual worship services or meditation sessions, may not fully replicate the sense of community and personal connection found in traditional settings. The challenge lies in balancing the convenience of digital access with the need for authentic and meaningful spiritual experiences.

The Intersection of Spirituality and Science

The relationship between spirituality and science reflects a dynamic interplay between different ways of understanding the world. While science provides empirical insights into the nature of reality, spirituality offers perspectives on meaning and transcendence that complement scientific knowledge.

1. **Complementary Perspectives:** Spirituality and science can offer complementary perspectives on existence, purpose, and the nature of consciousness. While science focuses on understanding the physical and empirical aspects of reality, spirituality explores the subjective and existential dimensions of human experience.

   o **Example:** The study of consciousness in neuroscience and psychology can intersect with spiritual practices that explore the nature of awareness and self. Insights from both fields can contribute to a more holistic understanding of human experience.

2. **Dialogue and Integration:** The dialogue between spirituality and science can foster mutual enrichment and understanding. By integrating insights from both domains, individuals and communities can develop more comprehensive and nuanced perspectives on reality and existence.

   o **Example:** The field of neurotheology explores the intersection of neuroscience and spirituality, investigating how spiritual experiences and practices may influence brain function and well-being. This interdisciplinary approach can enhance our understanding of the relationship between spirituality and cognitive processes.

Spirituality and Ethical Living in the Modern World

In addition to addressing personal meaning and purpose, spirituality can also inform ethical living and social responsibility. Spiritual values and principles often intersect with broader ethical considerations, guiding individuals in their interactions with others and the world.

1. **Ethical Principles and Practices:** Spiritual traditions often emphasize values such as compassion, empathy, and justice. These values can inform ethical decision-making and behavior, guiding individuals in their personal and social interactions.

   o **Example:** Many spiritual traditions advocate for environmental stewardship and social justice, encouraging individuals to act in ways that promote the well-being of the planet and its inhabitants. These principles can guide efforts to address global challenges such as climate change and inequality.

2. **Spirituality and Social Responsibility:** Spirituality can inspire individuals to engage in social and community-oriented activities that reflect their values and contribute to the common good. By integrating spiritual principles into social action, individuals can work towards creating a more just and compassionate world.

   o **Example:** Spiritual organizations and communities often participate in charitable and advocacy efforts, such as providing aid to those in need or advocating for human rights. These actions reflect the commitment to ethical living and social responsibility that many spiritual traditions uphold.

Spirituality in the age of doubt offers a profound source of guidance, comfort, and meaning amidst the complexities of modern life. As traditional structures of belief and practice face scrutiny and transformation, spirituality evolves to address contemporary challenges and aspirations.

By exploring the nature of spirituality in modern times, addressing existential questions, and integrating spiritual practices into the digital and scientific landscapes, individuals can find ways to navigate uncertainty and cultivate a deeper sense of connection and purpose. Spirituality provides valuable resources for coping with life's challenges, fostering ethical living, and enriching our understanding of ourselves and the world.

As we continue our exploration of doubt, certainty, and meaning, the role of spirituality highlights the enduring quest for transcendence and the search for deeper understanding amidst the evolving landscape of contemporary life. Through personal reflection, spiritual practice, and ethical engagement, we can navigate the age of doubt with resilience and insight, ultimately finding a sense of fulfillment and purpose in an ever-changing world.

Chapter 14: Self, Identity, and the Uncertainty of Being

The question of "Who am I?" has echoed throughout human history, as individuals seek to understand the essence of their identity. In the age of doubt, this inquiry becomes even more complex, as traditional frameworks for defining the self are increasingly challenged by societal changes, cultural shifts, and advancements in science and technology. In this chapter, we explore how the concepts of self and identity are shaped by uncertainty, delving into the philosophical, psychological, and existential dimensions of what it means to be.

The Fluidity of Identity in a Changing World

Identity, once thought of as a relatively fixed construct, is now recognized as fluid and multifaceted. It is shaped by personal experiences, social contexts, and cultural forces, all of which are subject to change. This fluidity introduces a sense of uncertainty, as individuals continuously reassess and redefine who they are.

1. **The Influence of Social Constructs:** Identity is often influenced by societal expectations and cultural norms. Categories such as gender, race, nationality, and social class contribute to how individuals understand themselves and are perceived by others. However, these categories are not static; they evolve over time and are subject to reinterpretation.

   o **Example:** The growing recognition of non-binary and gender-fluid identities challenges traditional binary conceptions of gender. This shift reflects a broader understanding of identity as a spectrum rather than a fixed category, inviting individuals to explore and express their gender in ways that resonate with their personal experiences.

2. **Identity in the Digital Age:** The rise of digital technologies has further complicated the concept of identity, as individuals navigate multiple selves across online and offline spaces. Social media platforms, in particular, offer opportunities for self-expression and identity experimentation, but they also introduce new forms of uncertainty.

   o **Example:** On social media, individuals curate their identities, often presenting idealized versions of themselves. This can create tension between one's public persona and private self, leading to a sense of disconnection or uncertainty about one's true identity. The pressure to conform to social media norms can further exacerbate this tension.

Philosophical Perspectives on the Self

The philosophical inquiry into the nature of the self has a long and rich history, with thinkers across traditions offering diverse interpretations of what it means to be. These perspectives highlight the inherent uncertainty in understanding the self and the challenges of defining identity.

1. **The Self as a Social Construct:** Social constructionist theories argue that the self is not an inherent, unchanging entity but rather a product of social interactions and cultural contexts. According to this view, identity is continuously shaped by external

forces and is subject to change based on societal influences.

- o **Example:** The work of philosophers such as George Herbert Mead emphasizes the role of social interaction in shaping identity. Mead's concept of the "social self" suggests that individuals develop their sense of self through their relationships with others and their participation in society.

2. **The Fragmented Self:** Postmodernist thinkers challenge the idea of a unified, coherent self, proposing instead that identity is fragmented and multifaceted. This view reflects the complexities and contradictions of contemporary life, where individuals often navigate multiple, sometimes conflicting, identities.

- o **Example:** French philosopher Michel Foucault's work on the self explores how power, discourse, and societal institutions shape identity. Foucault argues that the self is not a fixed entity but rather a construct that is continually produced and modified through social and political forces.

3. **Existentialism and the Search for Authenticity:** Existentialist philosophers such as Jean-Paul Sartre and Søren Kierkegaard focus on the individual's responsibility to define their own identity in the face of uncertainty. For existentialists, the self is not

predetermined; it is something each person must create through their choices and actions.

- o **Example:** Sartre's concept of "existence precedes essence" suggests that individuals are not born with a pre-defined nature or identity. Instead, they must actively create their own essence through their decisions, even in the face of the inherent uncertainty and anxiety that comes with freedom.

The Psychological Dimensions of Identity

Psychology offers valuable insights into the processes by which individuals develop and maintain their sense of identity. These processes often involve grappling with uncertainty, as individuals navigate the complexities of self-concept, personal development, and social relationships.

1. **Identity Development and Crisis:** Developmental psychologists, such as Erik Erikson, emphasize the role of identity formation in human development. According to Erikson, adolescence and young adulthood are key stages for exploring and establishing a stable sense of identity. However, this process is often marked by periods of crisis and uncertainty.

   - o **Example:** Erikson's concept of the "identity crisis" highlights the internal conflict individuals face as they attempt to reconcile different aspects of their self-concept. This crisis is a normal part of development, but it can also lead to feelings of confusion and uncertainty about one's identity.

2. **The Self in Relationship to Others:** The concept of the "relational self" emphasizes the role of interpersonal relationships in shaping identity. According to this view, the self is not an isolated entity but is formed and re-formed through interactions with others.

   o **Example:** Psychologists such as Carol Gilligan have explored how gender and relationships influence identity development. Gilligan's work on moral development suggests that women, in particular, often define their sense of self in terms of their relationships and connections with others, which can lead to unique forms of identity uncertainty.

3. **The Impact of Trauma on Identity:** Psychological trauma can disrupt an individual's sense of self, leading to fragmentation and uncertainty. Trauma often challenges core beliefs about the self, others, and the world, prompting individuals to re-evaluate their identity in light of their experiences.

   o **Example:** Survivors of trauma, such as those who have experienced abuse or war, may struggle with a fractured sense of identity. The process of healing often involves reconstructing a coherent narrative of the self, integrating past experiences with a renewed sense of meaning and purpose.

The Role of Uncertainty in Personal Growth

While uncertainty can be unsettling, it also plays a crucial role in personal growth and self-discovery. Embracing uncertainty can lead to new insights, deeper self-awareness, and a more authentic sense of identity.

1. **Embracing the Unknown:** The process of identity formation involves venturing into the unknown and confronting uncertainty. By embracing uncertainty, individuals open themselves to new possibilities for growth and transformation, allowing for the development of a more authentic self.

    o **Example:** The concept of "liminal space," borrowed from anthropology, describes the in-between phase of transformation, where individuals are no longer who they once were but have not yet become who they will be. This space of uncertainty is often where profound personal growth occurs.

2. **The Role of Doubt in Self-Reflection:** Doubt is a natural and necessary part of self-reflection and identity exploration. By questioning assumptions and re-evaluating beliefs about the self, individuals can gain a clearer and more nuanced understanding of who they are.

    o **Example:** Philosophical traditions such as Socratic questioning encourage individuals to engage in self-doubt as a means of self-examination. This process of inquiry allows individuals to challenge their preconceived notions of identity and move towards a deeper sense of self-awareness.

The Search for Authenticity in an Uncertain World

In a world where identity is fluid and uncertain, the search for authenticity becomes a central concern. Authenticity involves living in alignment with one's true self, rather than conforming to external pressures or expectations. However, the quest for authenticity is often fraught with uncertainty, as individuals navigate the tension between societal influences and personal desires.

1. **Authenticity and Social Expectations:** The pursuit of authenticity often involves challenging societal norms and expectations. This can lead to feelings of uncertainty and alienation, as individuals must navigate the tension between their true selves and the roles they are expected to play in society.

   o **Example:** The pressure to conform to societal expectations around success, appearance, or behavior can lead individuals to suppress aspects of their true identity. The process of reclaiming authenticity often involves breaking free from these expectations and embracing one's unique qualities and values.

2. **Living Authentically in Uncertainty:** Authenticity does not imply certainty; rather, it involves embracing uncertainty as part of the human experience. By acknowledging the inherent

uncertainty of life, individuals can live more authentically, making choices that reflect their true values and desires, even in the face of doubt.

- o **Example:** The writings of existentialist philosophers such as Kierkegaard emphasize the importance of living authentically in a world filled with uncertainty. Kierkegaard argues that true authenticity involves embracing the "leap of faith" into the unknown, making choices based on one's own convictions rather than external assurances.

The uncertainty of being is an inescapable part of the human experience. As individuals navigate the complexities of self and identity in an ever-changing world, they encounter both challenges and opportunities for growth. The fluidity of identity, the philosophical and psychological dimensions of selfhood, and the quest for authenticity all highlight the central role of uncertainty in shaping who we are.

By embracing the uncertainties of identity and existence, individuals can engage in a deeper and more meaningful exploration of the self. Through self-reflection, personal growth, and the pursuit of authenticity, we can navigate the uncertainties of being with greater insight, resilience, and purpose. Ultimately, the journey of self-discovery is not about achieving certainty but about learning to live authentically in the midst of uncertainty, continually redefining who we are as we encounter new experiences and challenges in life.

Chapter 15: The Search for Absolute Truth: Is It Possible?

The search for absolute truth has been a fundamental aspect of human inquiry throughout history. From ancient philosophers to modern scientists, individuals have sought to uncover the ultimate realities that govern existence. However, the very concept of absolute truth is fraught with complexities and challenges. In an age where relativism, subjectivity, and cultural diversity increasingly shape our understanding of the world, the question arises: Is the search for absolute truth still viable? In this chapter, we explore the nature of truth, the philosophical and scientific quests to uncover it, and the limitations and possibilities that accompany such a pursuit.

The Nature of Truth: Objective vs. Subjective

At the heart of the search for absolute truth lies a tension between objective and subjective understandings of reality. Objective truth refers to facts and realities that are independent of individual beliefs, emotions, or perceptions. In contrast, subjective truth is shaped by personal experience, perspective, and interpretation. This distinction has long been a subject of philosophical debate.

1. **Objective Truth:** The concept of objective truth implies that there are facts or realities that exist independently of human observation or interpretation. This idea is often associated with scientific inquiry, where empirical evidence and reason are used to establish universal laws and principles.

   - **Example:** The law of gravity is often cited as an objective truth because it applies universally, regardless of personal beliefs or interpretations. It is a fundamental force of nature that can be observed, measured, and tested in various contexts.

2. **Subjective Truth:** Subjective truth, on the other hand, acknowledges that individual perspectives, emotions, and experiences play a role in shaping one's understanding of reality. In this view, truth is not a fixed or universal concept but is instead shaped by context and interpretation.

   o **Example:** Religious or spiritual beliefs often fall into the realm of subjective truth. For example, one person's belief in the existence of a divine being may be deeply meaningful and true to them, while another person may hold a different, equally valid perspective based on their own experiences and worldview.

The Philosophical Quest for Absolute Truth

Philosophers throughout history have grappled with the question of whether absolute truth exists and, if so, how it can be known. Different philosophical traditions have offered diverse answers to this question, each with its own implications for the search for truth.

1. **Plato's Theory of Forms:** One of the earliest and most influential attempts to conceptualize absolute truth comes from the ancient Greek philosopher Plato. In his theory of forms, Plato argues that the

material world is only a shadow of a higher, more perfect reality. According to this view, absolute truth exists in the realm of forms, which are ideal, unchanging, and eternal. The material world, by contrast, is subject to change and imperfection.

- o **Example:** Plato's famous allegory of the cave illustrates this idea. In the allegory, prisoners are chained in a cave and can only see shadows of objects projected on the wall. The shadows represent the imperfect and changing realities of the material world, while the objects casting the shadows represent the higher, unchanging truths of the realm of forms.

2. **Descartes and Rationalism:** René Descartes, a 17th-century philosopher, sought to establish a foundation for absolute truth through reason and rational inquiry. His famous dictum, *Cogito, ergo sum* ("I think, therefore I am"), reflects his belief that the existence of the thinking self is an indubitable truth. Descartes believed that by applying reason and skepticism, individuals could arrive at certain, objective truths about the world.

- o **Example:** Descartes' method of systematic doubt involved questioning all beliefs and assumptions until only those that were absolutely certain remained. Through this process, he concluded that the existence of the self (as a thinking being) was an undeniable truth, forming the basis for further inquiry into the nature of reality.

3. **Kant and the Limits of Human Knowledge:** Immanuel Kant, an 18th-century philosopher, introduced a critical perspective on the search for absolute truth. He argued that while we can know certain things about the world as it appears to us (*phenomena*), we cannot know the world as it is in itself (*noumena*). According to Kant, human knowledge is limited by the structures of perception and understanding, meaning that absolute truth may be beyond our grasp.

   o **Example:** Kant's *Critique of Pure Reason* challenges the idea that human reason alone can uncover absolute truth. Instead, he suggests that our knowledge is always mediated by the ways in which we perceive and process information, making it impossible to access the true nature of reality in its entirety.

The Role of Science in the Search for Truth

Science has long been regarded as a primary tool in the search for objective, empirical truth. Through observation, experimentation, and the application of the scientific method, scientists have sought to uncover the fundamental laws that govern the universe. However, even within science, the notion of absolute truth has been called into question.

1. **Scientific Theories and Falsifiability:** One of the key principles of scientific inquiry is falsifiability—the idea that a scientific theory must be testable and capable of being proven wrong. This principle, popularized by philosopher Karl Popper, suggests that scientific knowledge is always provisional and subject to revision in light of new evidence. As a result, science does not claim to offer absolute truths, but rather the best available explanations based on current evidence.

   o **Example:** The theory of relativity, proposed by Albert Einstein, revolutionized our understanding of space, time, and gravity. However, even this groundbreaking theory is not considered an absolute truth; it is a model that explains a wide range of phenomena, but it remains open to modification or replacement if new evidence emerges.

2. **Quantum Mechanics and the Uncertainty Principle:** In the realm of physics, the development of quantum mechanics in the 20th century further complicated the search for absolute truth. The Heisenberg uncertainty principle, for example, suggests that certain pairs of properties (such as position and momentum) cannot be simultaneously measured with perfect accuracy. This introduces a fundamental element of uncertainty into our understanding of the physical world.

- o **Example:** The uncertainty principle challenges the classical notion of deterministic laws governing the universe. Instead, it suggests that at the quantum level, reality is probabilistic and unpredictable, raising questions about whether absolute truth can ever be fully known in the realm of physics.

The Challenges of Relativism

In contrast to the search for absolute truth, relativism posits that truth is not fixed or universal but is instead contingent on context, perspective, and culture. This view has gained prominence in fields such as anthropology, sociology, and postmodern philosophy, where it is argued that different cultures and societies construct their own truths based on their unique experiences and values.

1. **Cultural Relativism:** Cultural relativism asserts that beliefs, values, and truths are shaped by cultural context and that no single culture's worldview is inherently superior to another's. According to this view, what is considered true or valid in one culture may not hold the same meaning in another, making the search for universal truths problematic.

   - o **Example:** Concepts of morality and ethics often vary across cultures. Practices that are considered morally acceptable in one society may be viewed as unethical in another. For instance, certain forms of marriage, gender roles, or religious rituals may be understood differently depending on cultural norms, highlighting the difficulty of establishing a single, absolute moral truth.

2. **Postmodernism and the Critique of Meta-Narratives:** Postmodernist thinkers such as Jean-François Lyotard argue that the search for absolute truth is inherently flawed because it relies on overarching meta-narratives—grand, universal explanations that attempt to account for all of reality. Postmodernism rejects these meta-narratives in favor of more localized, fragmented understandings of truth.

   o **Example:** Postmodernism challenges the idea that science, religion, or philosophy can offer a single, all-encompassing truth. Instead, it emphasizes the plurality of perspectives and the role of language, power, and context in shaping our understanding of reality. This view suggests that truth is always partial and contingent, rather than absolute.

The Possibility of Absolute Truth in an Age of Uncertainty

Despite the challenges posed by relativism, postmodernism, and scientific uncertainty, the search for absolute truth remains a central concern for many. While absolute truth may be difficult—if not impossible—to fully attain, some argue that it remains a worthwhile pursuit.

1. **Pragmatism and the Pursuit of Truth:** Pragmatist philosophers such as William James and John Dewey

argue that the value of truth lies in its practical consequences. According to this view, truth is not an abstract, fixed entity but is instead something that emerges through action, inquiry, and problem-solving. In this sense, the search for truth is an ongoing, dynamic process rather than a quest for an unattainable absolute.

- o **Example:** Dewey's concept of "truth as inquiry" suggests that truth is not something we discover once and for all, but something we actively create through experimentation, reflection, and adaptation. While we may never achieve absolute truth, we can continually refine our understanding and improve our ability to navigate the world.

2. **The Role of Faith in the Search for Truth:** For many, the search for absolute truth is not limited to reason or empirical inquiry but also involves faith, intuition, and spiritual belief. Religious and spiritual traditions often hold that absolute truths exist beyond the material world and can only be accessed through inner experience or divine revelation.

- o **Example:** In many religious traditions, the existence of a higher power or ultimate reality is considered an absolute truth that transcends human understanding. For believers, faith provides a way to connect with these deeper truths, even in the absence of empirical evidence or rational proof.

The search for absolute truth is one of the most profound and enduring quests in human history. Whether approached through philosophy, science, or spirituality, the desire to uncover ultimate realities reflects a deep-seated need to make sense of the world and our place in it. However, the challenges of relativism, uncertainty, and the limits of human knowledge complicate this search, raising important questions about whether absolute truth is attainable or even meaningful.

In an age of doubt, the search for truth may no longer be about achieving certainty but about engaging in an ongoing process of inquiry, reflection, and growth. While we may never fully grasp the absolute, the pursuit of truth—both personal and collective—can lead to deeper insights, greater understanding, and a more meaningful engagement with the complexities of existence.

Chapter 16: Conclusion: Living Between Certainty and Doubt

As we reach the conclusion of this journey through the realms of certainty and doubt, it becomes clear that the tension between these two forces is not just a philosophical problem but a central feature of the human experience. Throughout this book, we have explored how certainty provides comfort, structure, and stability, while doubt opens the door to questioning, creativity, and growth. Far from being mutually exclusive, certainty and doubt often coexist in a delicate balance, shaping the way we understand ourselves, the world around us, and the larger quest for meaning.

The Paradox of Certainty and Doubt

Certainty and doubt represent two sides of a philosophical coin. Certainty offers clarity, a sense of knowing, and a foundation upon which we build our lives. It gives us the confidence to make decisions, form beliefs, and navigate the world. Yet, too much certainty can lead to dogmatism, rigidity, and an unwillingness to question our assumptions or consider alternative viewpoints. It can close us off from the richness of experience, trapping us in fixed patterns of thinking that stifle intellectual and emotional growth.

On the other hand, doubt encourages us to ask questions, challenge norms, and explore the unknown. It pushes us beyond the boundaries of what we think we know and opens up new possibilities for understanding. Yet, living in constant doubt can be destabilizing. It can create feelings of uncertainty, anxiety, and paralysis, as we struggle to find solid ground in an ever-changing world. The key, then, lies in learning to navigate the tension between certainty and doubt—embracing the value of both while avoiding the extremes of either.

1. **The Role of Doubt in Intellectual Growth:** Doubt serves as a catalyst for growth, not only in the realm of personal development but also in the pursuit of knowledge. History shows that breakthroughs in science, philosophy, and art often arise from individuals who question established truths and dare to explore new ideas. From Galileo's challenge to the geocentric model of the universe to Einstein's revolutionary theories of space and time, doubt has driven progress by pushing the boundaries of what is known.

   o **Example:** The scientific method itself is rooted in doubt—hypotheses are tested, and theories are continuously revised in light of new evidence. This process reflects the dynamic nature of knowledge, where certainty is always provisional, and doubt remains a necessary tool for uncovering deeper truths.

2. **The Necessity of Certainty in Human Life:** While doubt is essential for growth, certainty provides the stability needed to live a coherent and purposeful life. In everyday existence, people rely on a certain degree of predictability and order to make sense of their experiences. Certainty helps individuals form identities, establish relationships, and make meaningful choices.

   o **Example:** In ethical decision-making, individuals often rely on moral principles that provide a framework for action. These principles, whether derived from religion, culture, or personal values, offer a sense of certainty that guides behavior and gives life meaning. Without this foundation, individuals might find themselves adrift in moral relativism, unsure of how to act or what to believe.

The Human Condition: In Between

Human beings are not meant to live entirely in certainty or in doubt. Instead, we exist in the space between these two forces, constantly negotiating the tension they create. This in-betweenness is both a challenge and an opportunity. It requires us to develop the intellectual and emotional flexibility to hold opposing ideas, embrace complexity, and find meaning even in the face of ambiguity.

1. **Embracing Uncertainty as Part of the Journey:** One of the key themes that has emerged in our exploration is that uncertainty is not something to be

feared or avoided but embraced as an inevitable part of life. As we have seen, some of the most profound philosophical and spiritual traditions teach us to live with uncertainty, recognizing that it is often in the unknown that we find the deepest truths.

- o **Example:** In Buddhism, the concept of "impermanence" underscores the idea that all things are in a state of constant change. This recognition of life's transitory nature encourages a form of spiritual acceptance—an understanding that certainty is an illusion and that peace comes not from clinging to fixed truths but from embracing the fluidity of existence.

2. **Certainty and Doubt in Personal Growth:** On a personal level, living between certainty and doubt means learning to trust ourselves while remaining open to growth and change. It involves cultivating both confidence in our beliefs and the humility to admit when we might be wrong. This balance is crucial for personal development, as it allows us to move forward with purpose while remaining adaptable and open to new experiences.

- o **Example:** Consider the process of self-discovery. At various stages of life, individuals develop certain beliefs about who they are, what they value, and what they want to achieve. These beliefs provide a sense of certainty and direction. However, as people encounter new experiences, challenges, and relationships, they may begin to question these beliefs, leading to moments of doubt and re-evaluation. This process of questioning is essential for personal growth, as it enables individuals to refine their sense of self and make more informed, authentic choices.

The Role of Meaning in Navigating Certainty and Doubt

One of the central questions explored in this book is how individuals find meaning in a world marked by both certainty and doubt. As we have seen, the search for meaning often involves a dynamic interplay between the two. Meaning is not something that can be fully grasped through certainty alone, nor is it something that emerges purely from doubt. Instead, it is something we construct through our engagement with both—through our ability to hold onto certain truths while remaining open to the possibility of change.

1. **Meaning as a Dynamic Process:** Rather than being a fixed or static entity, meaning is something that evolves over time. It is shaped by our experiences, our relationships, and our ongoing search for understanding. In this sense, meaning is not a final destination but a continuous process, one that requires us to embrace both certainty and doubt as part of the journey.

   o **Example:** Viktor Frankl, a Holocaust survivor and existential psychologist, famously argued that meaning is something we create in response to life's challenges. In his book *Man's Search for Meaning*, Frankl describes how individuals can find purpose even in the most difficult and uncertain circumstances. According to Frankl, meaning is not something that is given to us by the world; it is something we actively create through our choices and actions.

2. **Finding Balance in a Chaotic World:** In today's fast-paced and often chaotic world, the need for balance between certainty and doubt is more important than ever. The rapid pace of technological change, the rise of global challenges, and the increasing complexity of social and political issues all contribute to a sense of uncertainty. At the same time, the desire for stability, order, and meaning remains a fundamental part of the human experience.

   - **Example:** In the face of global uncertainty—whether due to climate change, political instability, or technological disruption—individuals and societies are often tempted to retreat into rigid ideologies or dogmatic beliefs. However, as we have explored, such responses can limit growth and close off possibilities for understanding. Instead, the ability to live with uncertainty, to question assumptions, and to remain open to new ideas is essential for navigating the complexities of the modern world.

Living with Certainty and Doubt: A Path Forward

The ultimate lesson of this exploration is that living with both certainty and doubt is not a contradiction, but a necessary part of the human condition. To live fully is to recognize the limits of our knowledge, to embrace the mystery of existence, and to find purpose in the ongoing search for understanding. It is to navigate life's challenges with both confidence and humility, holding onto the truths that guide us while remaining open to the possibility that those truths may change.

1. **The Role of Wisdom:** Wisdom lies in knowing when to trust our certainties and when to question them. It involves cultivating discernment—understanding that some truths are more reliable than others and that some forms of doubt are more productive than others. Wisdom is not about achieving absolute certainty or living in perpetual doubt; it is about finding the balance that allows us to navigate the complexities of life with grace, courage, and insight.

2. **A Life of Meaning:** In the end, the search for meaning is not about resolving the tension between certainty and doubt but about learning to live within it. It is about accepting that life is full of ambiguity and contradiction and that the path to meaning is not a straight line but a winding journey. As we move through life, we are continually called to re-evaluate our beliefs, adjust our perspectives, and seek new understanding. It is in this process that we find the true richness of the human experience.

Living between certainty and doubt is the essence of the human condition. It is a dynamic, ever-evolving state that requires us to embrace both the comfort of knowing and the freedom of questioning. As we navigate this tension, we discover that life's deepest meanings are not found in absolute truths or unwavering beliefs but in the ongoing process of exploration, reflection, and growth.

In the end, it is not certainty or doubt that defines us, but how we live in the space between them—how we balance the desire for stability with the openness to change, how we hold onto meaning in the face of ambiguity, and how we continue to search for understanding in a world that is always in flux. This is the challenge, and the beauty, of the human experience.